Light from the Cloister

By the same author

CALLED
*New Thinking on Christian
Vocation*

DAILY WE TOUCH HIM
Practical Religious Experiences

CENTERING PRAYER
*Renewing an Ancient Christian
Prayer Form*

CENTERED LIVING
The Way of Centering Prayer

A PLACE APART
*Monastic Prayer and Practice
for Everyone*

MONASTIC JOURNEY TO INDIA

THE EUCHARIST YESTERDAY
AND TODAY

IN PETER'S FOOTSTEPS
Learning To Be a Disciple

JUBILEE
A Monk's Journal

O HOLY MOUNTAIN
*Journal of a Retreat on
Mount Athos*

IN SEARCH OF TRUE WISDOM
*Visits to Eastern Spiritual Fathers
and Mothers*

CHALLENGES IN PRAYER

MONASTERY

LAST OF THE FATHERS

BREAKING BREAD
The Table Talk of Jesus

A MANUAL OF LIFE
*The New Testament for
Daily Reading*

MARY TODAY
*Challenging Woman, Model for
Maturing Christians*

THOMAS MERTON,
BROTHER MONK
The Quest for True Freedom

DAILY WE FOLLOW HIM
Learning Discipleship from Peter

PRAYERTIMES: MORNING–
MIDDAY–EVENING
*A Pocket "Liturgy of the Hours"
for All Christians*

A RETREAT WITH
THOMAS MERTON

LIVING OUR PRIESTHOOD
TODAY

THROUGH THE YEAR WITH
THE SAINTS
*A Daily Companion for Private
or Liturgical Prayer*

LONG ON THE JOURNEY
The Reflections of a Pilgrim

Light from the Cloister

by
M. Basil Pennington, O.C.S.O.

Photos by Paul Quenon, O.C.S.O.

Paulist Press ◊ *New York* ◊ *Mahwah, N.J.*

Book design by Theresa M. Sparacio.

Library of Congress Cataloging-in-Publication Data

Pennington, M. Basil.
   Light from the cloister by M. Basil Pennington; pictures by Paul Quenon.
      p. cm.
   ISBN 0-8091-3171-4
   1. Spiritual life—Catholic authors. 2. Laity—Catholic Church.
   3. Contemplation. 4. Retreats. 5. Cistercians—Spiritual life. I. Title.
   BX2350.65.P45   1991
   248.4'82—dc20   90-29006
                                                                            CIP

Published by Paulist Press
997 Macarthur Boulevard
Mahwah, NJ 07430

Printed and bound in the
United States of America

Contents

To
Aunt Katherine,
a most inspiring and dedicated
Christian layperson,
with gratitude and love

◊   ◊   ◊

When those who love God try to talk about him,
their words are blind lions looking for
springs in the desert.

—*Léon Bloy*

Foreword

*H*er appearance was startling, to say the least. Jesus and his twelve were reclining on divans, interspersed among the local notables, enjoying a hearty meal and some challenging conversation. Suddenly she was there. Certainly she was not overly dressed, this woman of the streets. Even those who piously averted their eyes were gripped by her extraordinary beauty. The perfumer in her hands caught their attention also. The practiced eye would have estimated its worth, if the exterior appearance did not belie the contents, at thousands of dollars—the finest thing from Damascus. With as much silence as grace, she quickly made her way to the feet of Jesus. Then all heard the crack. Instead of unloosening the elaborate stopper which would have allowed the rich contents to pour out extravagant drop by extravagant drop, Mary had broken the long neck of the alabaster jar and let the whole of its rich contents gush out on Jesus' feet. "The whole house was filled with the scent." As the magnificent heady odor reached their nostrils there was a corporate gasp. Judas gave it voice: "Why this waste?" Jesus would respond: "She has done a good thing."

Saint Joseph's Abbey
Spencer, MA

As Joe and Gail drove north along Route 31 across central Massachusetts, suddenly there came into their view the striking stone tower of the abbey. The sprawling buildings that hugged the top of the hill housed over a hundred monks, men from different parts of the United States and other parts of the world: carpenters, plumbers, electricians, bakers, nurses, doctors, lawyers and teachers and a good many priests. "Why this waste?" In this day when more and more parishes are without priests, when clinics for the poor are in desperate need of doctors, when Catholic schools are closing for lack of teachers—"Why this waste?" Men and women are wasting their lives within the cloistered walls of monasteries all over the Church. "Why this waste?" "They are doing a good thing," Jesus replies. "The whole house of the Church is filled with the scent."

Most monks and nuns do not feel too comfortable with the "monastery as powerhouse" analogy made popular by some of the great preachers of the past. It conveys far too materialistic a notion of that gracious divine activity among and within God's people that we call grace. But they are keenly aware of the oneness they have with every human person and the even more intimate oneness they have with each one baptized into Christ. They know that their own daily struggle to enter more fully into the divine draws with them all their sisters and brothers in the human family and especially those within the communion of the Church.

Besides this deep interior reality that affects lives so hiddenly, when monks and nuns gather to establish monasteries they create a special place apart to which their sisters and brothers who are more immediately engaged in the activities of the Church in the world can withdraw when they feel the need to find a refreshing repose. A monastery is always there for others, for all the People of God, for the whole human family.

It stands there, too, to bespeak a message—an eloquent signboard along the side of life's road. It says something about God being worth it all. God is God. He rates all we have. He has given it all to us. But the wonder of our God. He has given it to us for our happiness, or rather so that we can share his happiness, divine, infinite, unending happiness. Monks and nuns are fortunate ones who have been invited to begin even now to share that happiness and do nothing else. They have been invited to the "paradise" of the cloister. Unfortunately, the one they bring into this paradise, namely themselves, is not quite ready for paradise. And so they know much of the struggle and pain of their brothers and sisters who are making the same heavenward journey out on the highways and byways of the world. The monk's life apart, therefore, inculcates and seeks to live out the same basic values that must mark the life of every Christian. This, too, is part of the message they have for the rest of the Pilgrim Church.

Now I invite you, with Joe and Gail, to turn off the highway and drive down into the valley past Lac Marie and up the hill to the abbey. After a brief pause in the quiet dark church for a prayer to the Holy Spirit that she might be with us, let us settle down in the comfortable warmth of the guesthouse and reflect together on some of the basic values of the Christ-life which we share. We will talk a bit about the way monks and nuns seek to live them out. This will perhaps help us to understand them a little better. Then we will explore ways in which you might practically incorporate them more richly into your life as you continue along life's journey.

Before beginning our discussion, I would like to thank all those who have actually sat with me around our large fireplace and explored these values with me. These friends have given me as much if not more insight than they received. To them much of the following is due. I also want to thank my brother monks who have received me not only as a passing guest but as a brother and have supported me in my poor efforts to live these values ever more fully. And a special word of thanks to Paul who has contributed the pictures that add so much to this volume. I count on the Lord to pay all my debts.

I am conscious, as we begin to share, that the monastery is Mary's. She is here mothering us, mothering the Christ in us, in response to his dying wish. I place these pages, and you, dear Reader, into her loving hands.

Father M. Basil, O.C.S.O.
Assumption Abbey, Ava, Missouri
Feast of the Assumption, 1989

Going Apart

I stood in the wheelhouse of Waterman Lines' largest freighter. We had been on the sea for over ten days and were now entering the harbor of Barcelona. I was fascinated by the radar screen, for in the darkness we could see little, yet it showed much. Just west of the city it picked out the mammoth granite stalagmites that jut up from the plains of northern Spain. This was the Montserrat, atop of which stood a large historic Benedictine abbey. It would take our car hours to wind around and around the perilous mountain road until we reached the stunning heights.

Monks reach for the heights. They also seek their apartness in other ways. Sergius Bolshakoff describes his visit to Uusi Valamo, a monastery in Finland:

> Our small boat nosed its way through the bewildering succession of lakes of northern Saimas. The further we moved to the northeast, the wilder and emptier the country became. Tall and silent forests lined the shores of the lakes through which we were pass-

Hermitage
Assumption Abbey
Ava, MO

ing. Hardly any dwellings or fields were to be seen. The region is all forest, bathed in silence and solitude.

But one does not have to go to the heights or the depths to find a place apart. Anyone who has penetrated an inner city Carmel with its high walls, its grills, and its curtains, knows how much even in the midst of a teeming city a monastic community can set itself apart and create a climate of apartness.

That is the important thing, the sense of apartness. The heavenly voice said to Arsenius, the praying courtier, "Flee, be silent, pray." And the palace favorite made his first step toward becoming a desert father. If one note is characteristic of the true monk it is this: he is the one who has gone apart, to be in some way alone—*monos*, alone, one with God. Gone apart to find silence to pray, to commune with God.

The follower of Christ, the Christian who wants to follow Christ, to live the Christian life to the full, not so much extensively in activities as intensively in act, remembers how often his Master went apart to pray. Jesus' years of growth were so hidden, we know virtually nothing of them. After he received his commission to ministry through a voice from heaven: "Listen to him," he disappeared into the desert for weeks of solitude and silence and, we may be sure, prayer. As his busy years of healing ministry unfolded, again and again, alone or with his chosen friends, he went apart:

9

When Jesus received this news [of John the Baptizer's beheading] he withdrew by boat to a lonely place where they could be by themselves. (Matt 14:13)

After sending the crowds away he went up into the hills by himself to pray. (Matt 14:23)

Six days later, Jesus took with him Peter and James and his brother John and led them up a high mountain where they could be alone. (Matt 17:1)

The apostles rejoined Jesus and told him all they had done and taught. Then he said to them, "You must come away to some lonely place all by yourselves and rest for a while." (Mark 6:30)

The monk goes apart in imitation of his Master and primarily for the same purpose as his Master: to be one with him in communion with the Father. The monk seeks to be alone—all one—at oneness with all, in that oneness we find in God. He has had some intimation of the reality of baptism, that he has been made one with the Son. His whole movement is to the Father in the Son through the Holy Spirit, conscious that in Christ he is one with all, that his movement with Christ's has a universal mediatory role.

"The fascination of trifles obscures the good," says the Wise Man. It is difficult in the midst of much doing and seeing to keep alive and present to the deepest reality, to the really real. And so the monk goes apart to find a greater quietness, a daily sameness, a stability that forestalls some of the onrush of new sights and sounds. He can, of course, bring distracting things with him into his solitude. He will bring much with him—all he has ever experienced—in his memory. And it will give him lots of replay. He will have to learn to turn off that inner dialogue; or better, to sink to the deeper places where its frequency is unattuned; or best, to integrate it into the growing harmony that allows all to speak of God and to God in him.

His solitude, his apartness, allows him to gain that perspective on himself and then on the rest of creation that leads to such an integration. Isaac of Stella, a twelfth-century Cistercian abbot, speaking of the Master's going up on a mountain, comments, "My Lord Jesus, and perhaps he alone, can in a crowd not be distracted by the crowd from seeing the crowd." But it is only the person "who sees the crowd well, who can fully turn from its attractions, easily go out from it and freely forget it."

Distance is needed for perspective and true spiritual freedom. But the solitude we most seek and for which this physical and inner solitude is a prepara-

11

tion is the solitude to be found in God. Of this solitude, Saint Bernard, the saintly abbot of Clairvaux, exclaimed: "O blessed solitude, my sole beatitude!" Of this solitude I really cannot write. It is to be experienced. It is so solitary, there is nothing of which to write. Yet, in this solitude, all is. And one knows in this solitude that he has in the power of God, in the Christness of his person, the love power, the being to lift the whole creation. And, in fact, in his very being there he is lifting up the whole creation, every woman, man and child, and all else, animate and inanimate. In his solitary kiss of the divine, in entering into the embrace of God, he brings all forward, a stride closer to the fullness and consummation that comes about from the creation's receiving in fullest freedom the fullness of the embrace of Divine Creating Love.

The call to solitude, to know and enjoy a certain amount of physical solitude, and certainly, to enter into the solitude of God, is not the exclusive prerogative of the monk (even though it might be the essential characteristic of his particular vocation). When I think of the role of solitude in the life of the active person, the name (though there are many) that most immediately and prominently comes to the fore in my mind is that of the great Father of India, Mahatma Gandhi. Father, grandfather, lawyer, statesman, activist, pacifist, his life could not have been fuller, and yet it was a life that always found time for solitude.

Even when the whole of the subcontinent awaited his every word and the future of this people and his nation hung upon him, or because of this, each week Gandhi faithfully took a day apart and entered into silence and solitude. In the light of such an example, what person can say that she or he cannot afford to take time for apartness—indeed, who can afford not to take time for apartness?

Gandhi was a man of such power because he was sourced. He was a man of such clarity and perspective because he regularly went apart. He accomplished so much for his people and was such a realized and complete person himself because he acted first for God.

> I can testify that I may live without air and water, but not without Him [God]. You may pluck out my eye, but that cannot kill me. You may chop off my nose, but that cannot kill me. You blast my belief in God and then I am dead.

Certainly we are not all called to be another Gandhi. But we all do want to be powerful—powerful in ways of life and love, calling others forth to fuller life and love. We all do want to be fulfilled and realized persons, living according to our own fullness, finding therein the joy, the peace, the happiness for which God has made us. To do this, to keep perspective, to be sourced, to be in harmony with who we truly are, we have to go apart, according to our own needs and rhythm.

We do not all have the flexibility in our lives to be able to make the time and establish the space for a weekly day of apartness. But let us be very realistic here. There is in the lives of most of us a good bit more freedom and flexibility to organize such a dimension *if we really want to.* In setting about integrating the values of apartness into our lives this would be the first question: Do I see a real value in having regularly a time apart? At this point I hope you will answer, yes. But for many this might still be more an intellectual conviction of variable strength than an experiential knowledge that amounts to almost a physical hunger. I recall a line from a letter of a friend speaking of this: "As for the time apart, all I can say is that when I miss it, I miss it." Well said!

Do I really want time apart? Do I know I need time apart? I do make time and place for what I want, what I need. A couple of friends proudly showed me through their new home. Prominent in the tour was their prayer room. I dare say that five years earlier, if this same couple were setting up that house, that little room would probably have been a study or a guest room. But they had come to know the importance of apartness in their lives, even their daily lives, and they made a place for it.

I think to have a place for this apartness is important. I speak of it even before the question of time because, making the time (note: I say "making the time"—we don't just "find" it), we have to have some place to spend it. Moreover, a constituted place stands there beckoning to us, reminding us to make the time. Probably very few will be able to use a whole room in their home exclusively as a place for apartness, for prayer and solitude. Yet I believe more homeowners than one might first suspect will be able to do this and will do it, once they have reconstituted their hierarchy of values and readjusted their living space accordingly. For most, the at-home place apart may well have to be an alcove, a dormer, a closet, a corner of their room or some less used room. A shrine of sorts will mark it off from the space around it, will proclaim a Presence, a place of encounter. Everyone has personal tastes and attraction. It is interesting to look into the cells (as monks call their rooms; it has nothing to do with prison cells. "Cell" comes from the Latin word *cella*, related to the word *coelum*, heaven, the place where one enjoys God) around our monastery. One, in the style of Eastern Christian homes, has a large shrine of icons opposite the entrance, a lamp ever burning before them. In stark contrast to this, another cell is completely nude. An expansive lightsome wall speaks powerfully of divine solitude. Another boasts but an empty cross, inviting ascension, transfixion and transformation. Most cells have the Bible enthroned, and in some this is the centering presence of the place apart. One has a rich collection of relics—the saints are there to support the solitary. To each his own. The important thing is that there is this place which, when one goes there, even if the going is no more than turning one's chair around, one has a sense of having gone apart.

If one cannot find such a niche anywhere at home—and that may very well be the case in many instances—then one has to look further afield, perhaps to a nearby church or chapel. A friend in Washington has arranged with a community of sisters a few blocks from his apartment to slip into their usually empty chapel. Most pastors are quite willing to give a church key to a sincere prayer for off-hour use. One might find a park, a library, a museum. Thomas Merton, during a certain period in New York, found his place apart at The Cloisters museum. A businessman might create his prayer corner in his office. A car has been a hermitage for many. Each one who wants to will find his or her place near at hand for daily apartness and will make the time to enter into that place.

And each will have her or his own rhythm. The times of sunrise and sunset, morning and evening, sacred to almost all traditions, may have difficulty fitting into the pattern of some lives. Moderns hardly live by the sun. Electricity turns night into day. Maybe it is a bit of our perversity that even as tykes we want to stay up as late as we can and get up as late as we can. At first, rather naked conviction and discipline may have to carve out our time apart with a certain amount of loving ruthlessness—both in regard to ourselves and in regard to others. Don't be afraid to experiment with times and rhythms. But seek to come to discover, perhaps with the help of your spiritual guide or friend, what really works for you. By that I mean how much time apart you need to keep true perspective, to be truly sourced, to experience in your life in an abiding way the fruits of the Spirit: love, joy, peace, patience, kindness, benignity.

For some, the rhythm may not be daily, or the daily time apart minimal. Larger spaces and other intervals will be more important. For all, though, the daily time apart will not be sufficient. There will need to be periodically more significant times if you are to derive the full benefit of this value. The couple whom I mentioned above, who have a prayer room in their home, do nonetheless seek out a house of prayer near the abbey for a monthly time apart. Others come to the abbey itself for their weekly or monthly day apart. For most there is some retreat house, monastery, or house of prayer within reach where they can find a place apart for more significant sourcing. However, if age, sickness, disability or some other factor prohibits, they may just have to close the door of their room for a day and make the daily place apart special in some way. Again, too, the rhythm will be according to each one's needs and attractions. A day a month, a week a year is common, but not all that common. Find what really works for you.

There is something of the monk in each one of us. Not to be neglected in this apartness is that

17

precious cell in the heart. There is deep within us a place apart. Perhaps if we begin to explore it, we will discover we have made it into a bit of a storeroom. Perhaps it is even so crammed with junk we can hardly get in or close the door. Saint Benedict in his Rule reminds monks: "The oratory should be what it is called—a place of prayer. Let nothing else be done or kept there." We may have to do some housecleaning. But we do have this place within where we can at any moment retire, close the door (as our Lord said) and enjoy for that moment a place apart. Get to know that inner cell. You will come to love it and it will come to be a true friend. When you are harassed or weary you will begin to experience it reaching out to you, beckoning: Come apart and rest awhile. In its deep, cool darkness, sometimes illuminated by a light not of our making, a moment can be a refreshing step into eternity, a coming home to the solitude of God.

"A place apart"—there are many places apart for each one of us: those we create, those we find, those created for us. Each is a gift and has its gifts for us. Seek and you shall find. Taste and see!

Into the Silence

The sun would soon rest on the horizon. The flood
tide of a day's activities is eddying. A calm enfolds
the abbey as a great cowl. The monks silently gather
in the reading cloister along the south wall of the
church. A junior reads a few pages from the sayings
of the desert fathers:

> Theophile of holy memory, Bishop of Alex-
> andria, journeyed to Scete, and the brethren
> coming together said to Abbot Pambo: Say a
> word or two to the bishop, that his soul may
> be edified. The elder replied: If he is not edi-
> fied by my silence, he will not be edified by
> my words.

Tu autem. The abbot gives the signal to conclude
the reading. "And you . . . Lord, have mercy on us."
The "Thanks be to God" comes from deep within the
monks. Another day is drawing to a close—a blessed
day, for his mercy has been with them. They silently
file into the church and into their choir stalls. The bell
rings and the ancient service of Compline proceeds.
Finally, the lights fade. Two solitary candles shadow

Cloister shrine
Redwoods Abbey
Whitethorn, CA

the folds of her mantle and caress the smooth cheeks of the medieval Madonna, the Queen of Cîteaux. And the monks' voices rise in the plaintive chant:

Hail, holy Queen, Mother of Mercy, our life, our sweetness and our hope. . . . O clement, O loving, O sweet virgin, Mary.

The final strokes of the angelus bell lose themselves in the surrounding hills. The monks bow, one by one, to be washed again with the baptismal waters and sent into the night with their abbot's blessing. Night has come. The "great silence" has taken hold of the abbey.

Creation has given up its activities and is hushed. It is time for the monk who has entered into God's established rhythm to be quiet and rest.

For many, when they think of monks they think of silence. I cannot say how many times I have been asked: Do you still have a vow of silence? Actually Trappists have never taken a vow of silence. Few monks have. Perhaps the most famous is the great icon painter Roublev. It was during fourteen years of vowed silence that he produced some of his greatest works. Silence had released his creative genius.

We do not have a vow of silence but we do have important rules of silence in the monastery. They are essential if a group of persons is going to live together and still have the context in which truly to seek God.

One of my favorite biblical scenarios (I have

many) concerns the holy prophet Elijah. He was a sporting man and challenged the false prophets of Baal to a contest. They gathered on Mount Carmel, each with his altar and holocaust. The Baalites cried all day for fire from heaven and Elijah goaded them on with his stinging jibes. Needless to say, no fire came. Then Elijah soaked his offering and altar with water and filled the trench around it with more of the same. Then he raised a single cry to heaven. Fire not only consumed the holocaust, it took the altar, too, and lapped up all the water in the trench. The crowd was ecstatic, and, encouraged by the holy prophet, proceeded to slit the throats of the false prophets. A bit of excessive zeal, we might say. The queen felt that way and promised Elijah the same fate. He made for the desert. A discouraged man—his great triumph had landed him in exile—he lay beneath a scrubby tree and complained to God as he fell into sleep. The Lord had something to teach his sporting prophet. An angel poked him, fed him, and sent him on a forty-day hike to the holy mountain of Horeb. The prophet found himself a cave and waited upon the Lord. A mighty wind tore the mountain and shattered the rocks. But the Lord God was not in the wind. There was a violent earthquake and Elijah shook. But the Lord was not in the earthquake. Fire blazed up and around and came down. But the Lord God was not in the fire. Then came a sound as if a gentle breeze.

When Elijah heard this, he covered his face with his cloak and went out and stood at the entrance of the cave.

The Lord God was in the gentle breeze, in the sounds of silence. Elijah learned to cloak himself in silence to hear the Lord. This is the deepest reason for the monk's silence, whether it is the "great silence" of the night which enfolds his sleep and his watching or the spaces and places of silence he guards in the day. It is to hear God. It is to tune out others for the moment so he can tune in God. "Be still and know that I am God."

God does indeed speak to us through all the events of life, through all the persons we encounter. He is actually in the mighty wind, the earthquake, the fire, in all. But we will not hear him in any of these— not even in the voice and embrace of a lover, if in the silence we have not learned the sound of his voice. It is very subtle, even though it thunders louder than all the voices of his creation. Two could be sitting in the warm sun, listening to the bright morning calls of chickadees, robins, finches and sparrows. One might only hear the rich melodies while the other, who perhaps has sat that morning in the silence and had attuned his inner ear to the divine voice, hears a message of ineffable love: Listen to the birds of the air. They do not sow or reap or gather into barns yet your heavenly Father feeds them. You are worth more than many sparrows. You are held in an infinite caring love.

In the silence, whether we listen to the creation around us, the words of revelation, or the deepest stirring of our own hearts, we begin to perceive another voice, one that is too often lost in the static of life. It is no use saying: "Speak, Lord, your servant wants to hear," if we never risk the silence to listen. If we never sit still we will never perceive the gentle breeze that caresses our necks and kisses our checks with love—a divine love.

In the spaces of silence the monk hears God, is embraced by God, delights in God. No wonder he is a lover of silence. He also hears someone else. He hears himself—his true self.

Happiness consists in knowing what we want and then knowing that we have it or are on the way to getting it. Most people are unhappy because they do not know what they want. This not knowing is partially a failure to choose. God does give us an immense amount of options from which we can choose. Some refuse to choose or find themselves paralyzed in the face of choice, because to choose one thing means to give up some others. But even those who do choose are often unhappy because the choice is not responsive to their own deepest needs and desires. We have to know ourselves in order to know what we truly want. Ultimately, it is only when we see ourselves reflected back in the all-loving eyes of God,

when we hear him speak our name, that we truly know ourselves with our infinite potential for beauty, for life, for truth, for love. It is only then that we know our own awesome beauty, that we are worthy of the divine love because he has made us worthy. Only then do we know that "Our hearts are made for you, O Lord, and they will not rest until they rest in you." In silence we come to know ourselves and know what we truly want. And the doorway to happiness opens.

Unfortunately, in seeing ourselves as we truly are, not all that we see is beautiful and attractive. This is undoubtedly part of the reason we flee silence. We do not want to be confronted with our hypocrisy, our phoniness. We see how false and fragile is the false self we project. We have to go through this painful experience to come to our true self. It is a harrowing journey, a death to self—the false self—and no one wants to die. But it is the only path to life, to freedom, to peace, to true love. And it begins with silence. We cannot give ourselves in love if we do not know and possess ourselves. This is the great value of silence. It is the pathway to all we truly want. This is why Saint Benedict speaks of silence as if it were a value in itself: "for the sake of silence."

He notes, too, another aspect, quoting Sacred Scripture: "In a flood of words you will not avoid sin." Good communication is beautiful, it is precious. It is also relatively rare. If we feel we must fill all the time we have with others with chatter and even all the time alone with sounds of radio or television or the productions of our own minds or imaginations, we will be filled with lots of useless and even harmful words, thoughts, sounds and ideas. And our own contribution will be lacking in quality to say the least. How quickly we descend to gossip, to detraction, to calumny. To be together in silence listening to the many messages of divine love, to the message of divine love that we are to each other, can bond a relationship and be a far more meaningful and fruitful communication than most of our speech. Some years ago we received into our community for a week eleven Methodist ministers. As they were giving us feedback at the end of the experience the input of one of them touched me deeply. He said he was awed by the respect and trust we showed each other in the way we were together in the silence. The others agreed.

We do have rules of silence in the monastery. There are times of silence: the "great silence" of the night, the time of prayer, study, reading and rest. And there are places of silence: the cloisters, the reading rooms, the cells, and . . . These are essential if we are to live together in freedom. We have to have our mutual understanding and our commitment to them. If you want the value of silence in your life you will have to find or create places of silence, you will have to agree on times of silence. It might be an hour or two in the evening, or a few hours on Sunday afternoon when each is left free to read and pray, reflect and write. This is not impossible with children. They can be put to quiet games with themselves with their coloring books or blocks. For teenagers whose lives are encased in the ceaseless blare of a sound called music, to be given a structure to discover silence, to discover their true selves in a daily dose of silence can be a gift that is perhaps at first not welcomed, but for which as for dry wine, a taste develops that will last for a lifetime. The individuality of all children should be respected. If they cannot enter into the silence, they should be asked at least to respect the needs of others. Modeling by parents in this regard as in so many others is very important. The basic human need for balance between auditory stimulation and silence can be missed, becoming an unknown cause of much stress and strain.

A sort of great silence (according to the possibilities of a maturing family) in the home until the family gathers at the breakfast table can allow the daily routine of morning exercises, showering, and dressing to become a time for reflection and prayer. If we take a word from Scripture upon arising, it can be an accompaniment through the morning rituals and a touch-point for the whole day. Down in this part of the country they have the practice of using the "bed Bible." A Bible is left on the pillow (usually open to the place where one has last read) so that as one prepares for bed he has to pick it up and at that moment reads a verse to reflect on through the night. The Bible is then placed on one's shoes, so that when dressing in the morning, again the Bible is picked up and a verse is read to carry through the day. To take a couple of minutes when we first get out of bed to receive the rising sun or the setting stars can bring peace to the whole day. To take time to center for fifteen or twenty minutes after our exercises and shower can put us deeply in touch with God and self and solidly ground all the activities of our day, till we collect them all into the center at evening meditation.

The other side of silence is communication. These two are not wholly distinct. We can communicate by silence. Some of our best communication is in silence. Indeed as we have said, the primary purpose of silence is communication, to truly hear God, to hear ourselves and others and the whole creation more deeply. But there is a time to communicate in words, one of our precious human prerogatives. True communication is perhaps as rare or rarer than true silence. It, too, can and oftentimes should be fostered by some structures. Monasticism has its chapter meetings, its spiritual fathers and mothers, its traditional teaching on spiritual friendship. Marriage Encounter has offered the practical tool of "ten and ten." The spouses are asked each day to spend ten minutes writing to each other and ten minutes talking to each other of their relationship. Families need to schedule family meetings and decide really to talk to each other about the things that flow out of their being a family. Busy friends have to make time to be together in silence and in honest communication. There is a time for us to sit mentally with each friend, each member of our family, each member of our community, so that all can speak their being to us and we can check our response of love and care. I do this on my monthly retreat day.

Actually, true communication does not interrupt silence. As Thomas Kelly, speaking from Quaker silence, has so beautifully put it: "Words should not break silence, but continue it. For the Divine Life who was ministering through the medium of silence is the same Life as is now ministering through words." To put it another way, whether we be silent or whether we speak, it is the Divine Word we want to hear and to express. This is the silence of the cloister that is so full of love, joy and peace, of the presence of the Holy Spirit. "In silence, you shall gain your soul" and all else besides.

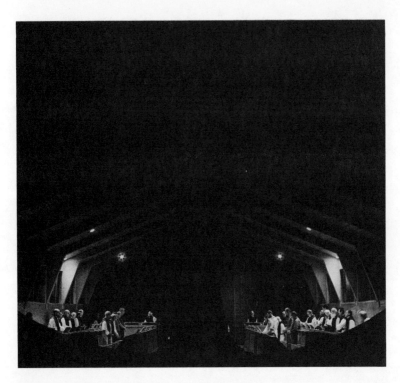

Choir at vigils
New Clairvaux Abbey
Vina, CA

Watch!

*D*ick snuggled down a little more deeply, tucking the blankets under his chin. The bells could not be said to have disturbed his sleep. Rather they invited him to enjoy it all the more, as he sensed himself embraced by the loving prayer of the monks and found a deeper sense of security. Perhaps when he first settled here thirty years ago to find work at the abbey as a carpenter the bells spoke more of material security. But now, especially in the last year since Ann died and he lay alone in his bed at night, the bells spoke deeply to him of another more important security. Even while the world around him slept, and he slept, he knew that he and his children and his grandchildren and all whom he loved were being embraced by the prayers of the monks in the night.

Across the fields, surely not more than three miles away, on the western slope, Claire, too, heard the vigil bell from the abbey. She rose quickly, wrapped herself in her ankle-length robe and set about stirring up the fire in the stove. Another log soon had it crackling and glowing, changing a cold dark room into a place of warmth and welcome. Claire had sought out and settled into this little cottage in the sight of the abbey and within earshot of the bells after having completed her twenty years as one of New York's "finest." The nearby monastery set the rhythm of her new life. She opened the folding door at the end of her room. As she lit the little oil lamps and the gilt background of each icon picked up the liveliness of the dancing flames, Claire found herself no longer alone. She was in the Presence of the Pantocrator, the Maker of All, and the Theotokos, the Holy Mother of God, and all her favorite friends among the heavenly court. She prostrated and her prayer rose like incense, one with the prayer of the monks in the abbey church, with monks and nuns everywhere and with all the solitary lay folk like herself who entered into this nocturnal praise.

Further down the hill, the bell gently intruded itself into the slumber of John and Maria. They said nothing, but drew more closely together and felt the beat of each other's hearts. They needed no words at this moment when their hearts rose together to the Throne of Mercy in a whole bouquet of sentiments: love, gratitude, petition, wonder, humility, and total being. Unlike Dick, who came here to work, and Claire, who came to retire, John and Maria had always been here. By American standards theirs was an old family, long farming the land. When rumor first told of the coming of the monks they had no idea what it might mean, but to these devout Catholics it sounded good. Now, John would be hard put to find quite the right words. He might more easily point to the more obvious effects. Not only he and Maria, but the children, too, had come to know the daily journey to the top of the hill for early mass. And there was a lot more prayer in the home. But it was more than that. The young ones might speak of it as the "vibes." Yes, the "vibes" had changed. There was a new peace upon the land, and it seemed more fruitful, too—at least to this experienced farmer. Something more than the sound of bells flowed out from the abbey on the hill.

On the crest of the hill, gleaming in the moonlight, the fieldstone abbey looked as if it had always been there—something that had naturally pushed itself up out of the soil, as indeed each of the stones had, before they were collected by the monks and brought together to create a twelfth-century abbey in twentieth-century New England. Inside its long, narrow church, the guest retreatants in the front and the hopeful candidates in the rear heard the bell, accompanied by the rustling of robes as the monks filled the stalls and then, standing as it were at attention, raised their voices:

O Lord, open my lips,
And my tongue shall declare your praise.

"Come, let us adore," sang the cantor. And the retreatants joined the monks in adoring, praising and thanking, the unspoken petitions in their hearts laid bare before their Father, not to be denied. The imagination of the candidates easily clothed them in the white cowl, set them in one of the stalls, repeating with all the choir: Yes, come let us adore!

In some reflective moments the monks were not unaware that the "vibes" of their prayer flowed out from the abbey not only into the immediate environs, but encircling the whole globe in a current of peace and caring love, uniting with the prayer of all and lifting up each one. But in the midst of the prayerful chant they were more conscious of the ascent to God, or rather of God himself and of all that ascended with their prayer. If challenged by questioning as to what they were about, they would not first think or speak of the empowering and uplifting, though they certainly would not deny it. Monks realize well that when the consciousness of one person is raised, the whole of humanity is raised; when the quality of life of one improves, all improve. Or, to put it in another, more biblical way, the increased health and vitality of any one cell vitalizes the whole Body of Christ.

But the monk might think more readily of Jesus and see his own rising in the night for prayer as an imitation, a following of his Master. At the significant moments of his life Jesus entered into a watch of prayer. As he inaugurated his healing ministry at Capernaum—

> In the morning, long before dawn, he got up
> and left the house, and went off to a lonely
> place and prayed there. (Mark 1:35)

When it came time to choose his apostles—

> He went out into the hills to pray; and he
> spent the whole night in prayer to God.
> (Luke 6:12)

The monk prays in the night in imitation of his
Lord and Master but also because it expresses the
very essence of his life. If we listen to what is deepest
in us we find a deep longing for God, a mind that
seeks all Truth, a desire to know that will be satisfied
only when it finds the ultimate Answer that ties everything together. And more important, more urgent,
and in the end more profoundly at the center of our
being, there is a heart that longs for a limitless love, a
heart that seeks that Love who is God Himself—the
only Love big enough to fill all our void. Indeed, if we
listen attentively we hear this seeking deep in every
human voice, see it in every human eye; we perceive
it in all the restless strivings of our sisters and
brothers. And in the rest of creation—the whole of
creation is in travail, groaning, seeking its fulfillment
in the fullness of the redemption that is to come to it.
One of the awesome models for monks is the

great Arsenius. We are told that as the sun set he raised his arms in prayer and did not lower them until the rising sun cast its shadow on the ground before him, when he prostrated before the Risen Son. Not many can approximate this holy monk's steadfastness. Even Moses had to be supported by Aaron and Hur as he watched through the day of battle. True, Christian monks in the Byzantine tradition do still watch through the night before Sundays and feasts. But Saint Benedict legislated for a weaker lot. He rouses his monks from bed at the seventh hour of the night (around two or three A.M.) after they are rested. But what else can one do at that hour of the night and in the subsequent hours but watch and wait for dawn? It is a time of seeking.

It may be that something deep within twists and stretches, taut with longing and expectation. Or the soul may lie as quiet as a dewdrop on the grass, crystallizing as it gathers in the light of the aurora until the first glint of the rising sun turns it into a fiery diamond to be laid in homage at the feet of the Risen Son.

On rarer occasions, the monk's watching is the bride's eager straining to catch a glimpse through the lattice of faith or the bridal party's excited listening for the footfall at the door. But even bridesmaids have been known to fall asleep in their watching. And so have monks. There will be those dull nights, when perhaps a damp chill will lie heavy, like fog, on the spirit and the thought of the great Arsenius will mock the flagging monk. If he is watching in his cell his eyes will cast furtive glances toward the inviting mattress in the corner. He may have to flee to the outdoors to let the rudeness of the night arouse him or else strain his weary muscles, rising and falling in prostrations until the heart pounds again to supply the holy exertions and irrigate the sluggish brain. More often it seems to be a bit of muddled reverie before the Lord or a quiet being-with a Loved One, a deep sense that this is right, that this is satisfying to some deep emptiness within. He is coming—it is good to be watching and waiting.

This experiential sense of watching and of the goodness of it usually does not come at once. The novice may be fortunate enough to have a period of honeymoon excitement when the watch is all sweetness and consolation. Or he may not. Soon enough it is fidelity to a practice, an observance, that carries the watcher on. But it is a fidelity that is in time rewarded. Maybe at first only sporadically, but in time it becomes a state of soul, something precious, not all that easy to describe, but precious and prized. It is a restive resting that has its painful delight. It is a time of love, a love more anticipated than experienced, perhaps, but a time of love—a very real "living with" an apparently absent and longed-for Lover. These hours of watching come to be among the most prized hours of the monk's day.

But to be practical, most "monks in the world" can hardly hope to adjust the clocks of their lives so as to be able to rise at the "seventh hour" of the night to enjoy a predawn watch. At best, with careful planning and the sure knowledge that there will be days when it just won't work out, one can plan to retire early enough to have a reasonable period (you will have to decide what might be "reasonable" for you: fifteen minutes, half an hour, an hour?) to "watch" before beginning other more formal morning prayer. It might be set off with lighting a candle or a bit of incense, a prostration before a holy image or the enthroned Scriptures, a reading from the Sacred Text or a psalm to rouse the spirit: Come, let us adore.

Some may find it of value and profit to have a more significant vigil once or twice a week, perhaps on Thursday night with Jesus in Gethsemane. This could take the form of rising a good bit earlier, sacrificing some sleep this one night or breaking sleep at the seventh hour to join in spirit with the monks and nuns in their monasteries. This might be easier on Friday night or early Saturday morning, when it would be possible to return to bed for a longer sleep. Missing sleep is not the important thing, though for some this can be a significant ascetical dimension of the practice. More important is the experience of being vigilant in the dark silence when others are not commonly abroad and even the creation has a certain dormancy. There is something about the deepness of that bottoming of nature's daily cycle (even in the city where it might still be punctuated by police sirens, the clatter of garbage collectors and the fights of alley cats) that opens out the deeper recesses of the spirit and lets its truer language surface. At such an hour what does creation do but await the sun? What can we do but await the Son?

> I wait for Yahweh, my soul waits for him—
> more than a watchman waits for the dawn.
> (Psalm 130:5–6)

The spirit of watching can be carried on beyond the actual time of prayer. As we shower, and dress we can continue to meditate on some Scripture text, repeat some simple prayer, or simply abide in the Presence, longing for an ever greater presence. A household agreement (something more possible when the children are grown) that allows this to be a time of quiet without chatter or the blare of radio, stereo or television would greatly facilitate this. The watch could formally be concluded with a bit of family prayer at the breakfast table. In my Uncle Clark's home we had a psalm, with a moment's reflection and a spontaneous prayer before we dived into our breakfast.

In reading the Fathers of the Church and our twelfth-century Cistercian Fathers, we repeatedly come upon the statement: "One who has experienced this understands what I am talking about; one who has not, let him seek the experience and then he will understand." When I was a young monk I used to be quite annoyed when I came upon such "snobbish" statements. Now I begin to understand. Anyone who has loved will. Just try to get another to understand what you experience in being with your loved one! The same is true here.

The value and effect of watching can only be known by experience. Even a little watching done regularly not only reveals its own significance, but has an effect on one's whole life. In the watching, new dimensions of the soul's natural magnetism toward the Lord begin to reveal themselves and the soul begins to have the joy of drawing the Lord into its cool darkness, radiating the warmth of unseen light. At the same time a certain integrity and unity seem gradually to take more and more hold of the multitudinous strands of life, creating a satisfying and empowering harmony. The whole comes more and more into harmony. The reasons for this could be explored at length: a purification process is being facilitated. The solitary perception is becoming more penetrating as these deeper openings are illuminated by the dark light. A freer, more vigorous spirit that has been strengthened to stand its ground in the struggle with darkness takes a firmer hold on the direction of one's life. The extensive effect of a relatively little investment of yourself and your time in watching will in many ways be surprising. The experience of it is in itself very rewarding and it is a constantly growing experience for those who are faithful to the practice.

Watch—and you will see!

And Listen

*I*n his Rule as he lays out the daily program, Saint Benedict allots rather large portions of time to *lectio*. The literal translation of this word is "reading" but in our Christian tradition it connotes much more. It refers to a whole method or way of spirituality which has often been summed up in the four Latin words: *lectio, meditatio, oratio, contemplatio*.

There are near our monastery two other monastic centers: the ashram of Swami Satchetananada and the Insight Meditation Center, a Theravada Buddhist community. Frequently young people, making the rounds, after visiting these neighbors will come to us. They will have experienced a bit of the eight limbs of yoga with the Hindus and some sitting with the Buddhists. Now they want to experience our thing. They ask: What is your method? I usually answer: The whole of our monastic life is our method. It is hearing the Word of God and keeping it. Whether we eat or drink or do anything else, we seek to do all for the glory of God. But if they press me, as they usually do, for something more specific, I say that *lectio divina* is at the heart of our method; then I seek to teach them

Meditative reading
Our Lady of Guadalupe Abbey
Lafayette, OR

how to hear the Word of God, meditate upon it, respond to it in prayer and rest in it in contemplation.

While it is probably true that Benedict's monks, like Basil's before him, were expected to learn to read, the ability to read was not a common attainment in Benedict's time or for long after. He received into the monastery some rather rough characters, the type who understood a beating better than wise counsel. Their reading ability was probably minimal. *Lectio* for Benedict and the early tradition had a broader connotation than simply reading. It meant receiving the revelation of God's love.

The place par excellence to receive this is, of course, the Sacred Scriptures. "I call you no longer servants but friends because I make known to you all that the Father has made known to me." In the Scriptures God reveals himself most intimately. The early monks often memorized large portions of these. Even when I entered the novitiate forty years ago we were expected to learn many psalms and readings by heart. For the monk, *lectio* might be calling up these texts from memory. It might be hearing another read. Frescoes, icons and later stained glass could be a source of *lectio*. Eastern Christian monks frequently stand before the holy icons and listen to them. In the Middle Ages the whole of the Scriptures found their way into stained glass. Today cassettes offer us a wonderful means whereby others can in a very living way share faith with us and open the Revelation or simply read the Scriptures to us while we walk, run, drive, bathe, shave, rest or work.

There are different kinds of sacred reading. We read to know—sacred study. It is important that we keep up our sacred study and keep our faith culture abreast with our secular culture. We read to act— spiritual reading; it is meant to motivate us, to influence the will. And there is *lectio;* it is meant to bring us into immediate communication with God.

God speaks to us more intimately through the Revelation, whether it reaches us in word or art or through the faith experience and commentary of his saints. As I write this I look out upon a magnificent landscape. A gentle wind moves the grasses to bow repeatedly to their Lord. The vast horizon tells me of his expansiveness. The songs of the birds echo our common cry to God. He who is invites me to an ever fuller share in his beauty. He lets his creation speak of himself and carry us beyond itself to him. For *lectio,* all creation is a book that speaks of God, and that is what we long to hear.

We hear the word and we want it to come alive in us to form us. The image may rest in our mind's eye and we enter ever more fully into it. Or the word may repeat itself again and again—not necessarily on the lips, though it might, but at least in the mind till it forms the heart. Early monastic meditation did not rely on a lot of thinking or on elaborated techniques as did later methods. The process was more receptive, allowing the revelation to form us and call us forth. This is *meditatio*.

The response to this is *oratio*, prayer. God's revelation can call us forth to many different responses. At times repentance is strong—our response has been so poor. Thanksgiving rises up—to a God so patient, so good, so generous. There is petition—we sense our needs. But ultimately, it is love longing for communion. And when this final disposition takes full hold of us it is *contemplatio*.

These are not so many stages along the way. It is true, at certain points in our life one or the other will prevail. And our constant tendency is toward the union of contemplation. But each day has its grace. One day we seem to read a lot, and nothing seems to call us forth. Another day we are as it were possessed by a word that repeats itself constantly. Some days we sense all reading and thinking as so much distraction; we simply want to rest in the Lord. A method like Centering Prayer can help us here.

As I have said, Saint Benedict allotted generous portions of the day to *lectio*. He was legislating for monks. A later writer, the author of *The Cloud of Unknowing*, undoubtedly a monk, writing for lay persons, spoke of periods of the day to be set aside. Most traditions have recommended two periods a day: one in the morning and another in the evening, at those cardinal points of sunrise and sunset—the empowering of a day's activity, the completing of a day's activity.

Most any text can be used for *lectio*. It is better if it is a text we are familiar with. Then we are not pushed on by curiosity to see what comes next. The Scriptures are by far the best text. Each will find the passages that best speak to him or her. For me it has always been the Last Supper discourse: John 14–16.

When we come to *lectio* the most important thing is our desire. The Lord will reveal himself and enter into our lives to the extent that we believe this is really possible and want it: "Ask and you shall receive, seek and you shall find." No one respects our freedom as completely as God does. "Behold I stand at the door and knock and *if* one opens I will come in." He never pushes the door open. He waits for us to open. This is what we do in our *lectio*—we open the door of our mind and heart for him to enter. And he will. If not precisely and experientially at the time of our *lectio*, then some other time, at a time perhaps when we least expect it and most need it. He has made us to be happy with him through an intimate union of love. He wants this even more than we do. He never lets our invitation go unanswered. He comes.

It is important to begin our *lectio* with an ardent plea to the Holy Spirit. "Eye has not seen, nor ear heard, nor has it entered into the heart of the human person what God has prepared for those who love him, but the Holy Spirit makes it known to us." "I will send the Holy Spirit, the Paraclete, who will abide with you. She will make known to you all that I have revealed to you." It is the Holy Spirit who inspired the Scriptures and the Fathers who have written on them out of their deep love and experience. It is she who dwells in us and will make them come alive in us. We depend upon her and should begin our *lectio* with a fervent prayer to her.

We may in our *lectio* just simply read and let the text speak to us as it will. We might even let the words quietly wash over us as we abide in our longing for God. Or we might more actively challenge the Lord and ourselves in the communication. Do we hear the Lord speaking in the second person or the third? Is he speaking directly to us or in general? Saint Augustine said of the psalms that they are speaking to us about Christ, or Christ is speaking to the Father or we are speaking to Christ. The Gospels and all Scripture can be taken in these ways, and others; especially can they be Christ speaking to us, calling forth our response. But we want to note here the difference between *lectio* and that spiritual reading which is aimed at motivating our life. In the case of the latter we do want to enter into a reflective process. We might ask ourselves such questions as:

Which person am I in the scene? Why?
What is so important about this event?

47

Where does this fit into all Jesus came
to accomplish?

Is there anything about Jesus here which especially draws me?

Is there any way he would like me to carry
on the work I see him doing here?

Is there anything here which tells me how I
could be more like him in the way I
look at life and people?

What has this to do with Church and society
today, with my family, community,
friends?

Does it make a difference?

Hearing the Scriptures this way can be very exciting
and it can change our lives. We do need to make time
for this kind of spiritual reading. But this is not precisely what *lectio* is about. *Lectio*, properly speaking,
does not seek information or motivation, it seeks communion and union. We are with the Lord and he
speaks to us in the language of Love.

It is the tradition, as I have said, to devote some
time regularly in the morning and evening to prayer.
In a gracious space the Word is more welcome to find
the time to unfold its mystery and lead us into the full
contemplative experience. We are incarnate persons,
so time and place are important. Besides these special
times with our Beloved, we can take moments in the
day to let him say a word to us. A small pocket Bible

or New Testament will allow us to receive a word while we wait in line in the bank or stop at a red light.

The method of *lectio, meditatio, oratio, contemplatio* is a very simple method and one that is most proper for the Christian. As Christians we are sons and daughters of the Book. It is our privilege to have received the Revelation. God has spoken to us. Most properly, then, is our prayer one of listening to God speaking to us and responding to that. For us all prayer, our very being, is a response to one who has first spoken to us in the creation—our own creation —and the Revelation. All that we are is response to his creative love. Using this method we make our times of prayer moments that fully embrace the reality, moments that fill us with great peace and joy. If you have practiced it you know what I am talking about. If you have not, then do it and you will soon know the experience. Listen and know that he is God, the God who loves you so, who loves you with an everlasting love and has prepared a place for you in his Kingdom.

Evening prayer
Christ in the Desert
Abiquiu, NM

The Work of God

I entered the monastery forty years ago. I remember well meeting Father Paul, the novice master. A brilliant man, a professor at Amherst before he donned the monastic habit, he had deeply sunken eyes that seemed to burn and sparkle. There was often a mirth in his caring love. He seemed to see through our novitiate confusions and bespeak assurance that it would all come out all right. He is well into his eighties now and still going strong, the same light and mirth in his eyes.

As he probed me that day and in the weeks and months that followed, he was gently but incisively exploring to see if I was truly seeking God, if I was growing in zeal for humility (I had a long way to go on that one—and still do), for obedience and for the work of God. For this is what Saint Benedict says the novice master should do.

To truly seek God—this is the every essence of monastic life, indeed of all Christian and Jewish life by precept and all human life by the very exigency of nature: Love the Lord your God with your whole mind, your whole heart, your whole soul and all your strength. This is first commandment. Monastic life means making this *the* thing of one's life. For us monks, the Lord is the love of our life. This is why we must be celibate—so that we can freely center all our being and love in God and with him share his concerned love for every one of his children, our sisters and brothers.

Concretely, for the daughters and sons of Saint Benedict this allness to God expresses itself in three interrelated concerns. We must be humble, setting aside our own ambitions, so that we can be a complete "yes" to God. We must be obedient, so that our whole being may be fully integrated into the divine plan. The passion of our lives must be that the work of God, his wonderful creation, his masterpiece, might obtain its ultimate meaning: to truly glorify its munificent and most loving Creator.

Often *Opus Dei*, the Work of God, is taken to mean the Divine Office, the services of praise that nuns and monks celebrate in choir. Indeed, Saint Benedict does take it in this sense, and this may be the primary sense for him. But these Offices have their meaning only because they are the key moments when the nun or monk lays aside all other activity to fulfill most solemnly his or her role as the high priest of creation, giving voice and heart to the rest of creation to praise its Maker. It is the moment when most precisely the work of God seeks to reflect back the glory of its Creator. It is at the Office, in the liturgy, that the creation attains its summit, its focal point.

Not only the monastic, of course, is called to this.

Every Christian who has been baptized into Christ shares in his priesthood, the High Priest of all creation. Every Christian is called to enter into his ultimate act of love and give to the rest of creation a divinized mind and heart with which to glorify the Maker. We need to let all the beauty, all the reality of God's creation enter into our hearts and then enfold it in our love so that it may ascend to him with that love. The Work of God, the Divine Office seeks to give voice to that ascension and effect it in the creation through us. The hours in choir are the high point of the monk's day but they will be the high point only if they are the expression of the basic attitude and activity of his whole day and life. His whole being is to be a "Glory be to the Father and to the Son and to the Holy Spirit."

Some years ago a controversy raged concerning the primacy of liturgy over contemplation. There were eminent theologians on both sides of the issue. Happily it petered out, and these men of learning went on to devote their time and talents to better ends. In fact, liturgy and contemplation are both expressions of the same basic attitude and movement of the Spirit.

"Contemplation" is an interesting word. It comes from Latin derivatives. "Con" means "being with": confraternity—being with the *fratres*, the brothers; communion—being in union with. "Tion" implies an "abiding state." So, "being with" in an "abiding state." Being with what? The *templa:* When the priests of ancient Rome sought to know the will of the gods, they searched the heavens; in particular they watched the flight of birds through a particular segment of the skies known as the *templa*. In time, the *templa* was projected on earth to become the *templum*, the temple, where people came to know the will of the gods, to enter into union with them. "Contemplation" is an abiding state of being with the will of God, the movement of God, of being with God Himself.

The liturgy is a school where through sign and symbol, word and music, our minds and hearts are formed to be in union with the movement of God, with God Himself.

The basic unit of the liturgy is the day. In the Jewish tradition it begins at evening. Early monastic communities separated from the evening prayer of Vespers, or the service of thanksgiving, another office which they called Compline, the completing service. It marks a completion: "Now let your servant depart in peace, O Lord." It is a dying: "Lord, grant us a peaceful night and a perfect death." It is a dying so that we may rise again. We go down into to the tomb so that we may share more fully in Christ's resurrection as the Son rises with the sun. The going down within the waters of Baptism and rising up out of them with Christ is renewed as the abbot sprinkles each monk with blessed water and sends him off to his cell. The monk will die to this world as he falls asleep. He may more radically die to this world as he watches in the night and is stripped of all consolation save the hope of the coming of the Risen Christ at dawn.

In the aftermath of the Second Vatican Council, liturgists sought to suppress Compline as a "later" innovation and a redundancy of Vespers. Two evening offices are not necessary, they said. At first the monks and nuns docilely accepted this but within a short time in many monasteries the Office of Compline returned. A deeper instinct prevailed. A basic element of Christian liturgy is this daily dying and rising with Christ; we need a completing office.

These are the basic Offices: Vespers-Compline, the dying, and Lauds, the rising with Christ, the coming of the Risen Lord into our day, our life. "Blessed be the Lord God of Israel, for he has come to his people . . . the tender mercy of our God who from on high brings the rising Sun to visit us, to give light to those in darkness and the shadow (or image) of death and to guide our feet into the way of peace." Watching is important for the nun and monk—the Vigils; but this may not be as easily incorporated into your life. The other Hours can more easily be brought in.

You can, of course, use the Office in an approved Book of Hours. These may seem long and complicated. I have prepared a very simple one for those who would want it: *Prayertimes: Morning—Midday— Evening* (Doubleday Image Book). If you cannot pray the whole of an Office, it is enough to pray what you can. You might prefer the Cistercian way. The Cistercians do not have a small office book, only the large books they use in choir. So when they travel they construct their own Office, using the Bible. Each hour is usually composed of a hymn, psalm(s), reading and prayer which may be quite spontaneous, flowing from reflecting on the reading.

A brief service of thanksgiving can perhaps be connected with your evening meal—before or after. This can easily make it a family or household celebration. A Compline prayer before retiring can be a most intimate moment of prayer for loved ones together. Light a candle before an image of our Lord and let the specialness of this completion of the day peacefully embrace you. Not much need be said: perhaps a psalm (I like Psalms 129/130, 130/131 or 90/91), a word from Scripture ("You are in our midst, O Lord; your name we bear. Do not forsake us, O Lord our God") and an Our Father or some spontaneous prayer, and then, if you will, a salute to Mary, the caring Mother: Hail, Holy Queen.

The morning prayer might be more personal: a morning offering, some inspiring reading, a time of silent meditation. I know a friend who listens to hymns and psalms on his cassette player while he showers and shaves to prepare for the reading and centering that will follow. You might find the chapel of your car a good place to celebrate Lauds and Vespers as you drive to and from work. Jogging provides another possible time and place. Some pray with recorded Offices from the abbey. Each individual or couple or household will find its own way to celebrate the resurrection and enter into the life of a new day with the Risen Lord.

Besides the basic rhythm of the day there is the rhythm of the week and year. I will say more about the week with its creative labor and Sabbath rest when I speak about our work.

The liturgical year invites us to enter into the full flow of salvation history. With the first Sunday of Advent we come out of chaos, look to an ultimate consummation and enter into the longing of a people for a Savior. When Christ does come at Christmas, we begin to live this central life of human history with him, first in large steps but as it nears its consummation, day by day, hour by hour in Holy Week until the liturgy comes to a halt on Holy empty Saturday. We need a night watch, a very full liturgy to enter into the Paschal mystery. "This is the night when heaven and earth are joined together." We live the joyful forty days of resurrection with Christ. We pray with Mary and the Eleven, awaiting the outpouring of the Spirit. We go forth with the Church carrying this whole created project with green hope toward the consummation when all will be Christ's even as he is God's. One of the liturgical reforms of the Second Vatican Council of which I am especially happy is the recognition of Thanksgiving as a full liturgical feast. As we lay all at the feet of Christ the King at the end of the year our hearts are necessarily filled with thanksgiving.

This re-presentation of salvation history in the liturgical year is not just a calling to mind, a symbolic drama; it is a real "making present." These events, all of them, exist now in God's eternal "now" and the liturgy brings them from his "now" into our time. Christ is really born on Christmas in sacramental mystery. It is a present reality. He lives his life, he dies, he rises, he ascends and sends his Spirit, he lives on in his Church. This is the reality of the people of God, those baptized into Christ. We want to enter fully into it.

Home liturgy can help. The Advent wreath can gather the household on the Sundays of Advent and remind them each day that he is coming. The grace of Christmas, the best of gifts, is something to look forward to. An empty crèche can heighten the longing of the last days of Advent until he comes. Epiphany can mean gifts to the Christs in our lives. Celebrating his baptism, the family can renew its commitment to one another in a renewal of baptismal promises. A household fast, if it be only from dessert on certain days, can make Lent more of a time with Christ in the desert. Each day can have its particular little acts of self-denial with alms for the poor, an offering to be brought to church on Holy Thursday. A Seder meal at home can make the Last Supper liturgy much more meaningful. Perhaps Jewish friends will grant you the privilege of joining in theirs or help you prepare your own. Each home should have its Paschal candle lit each time the household gathers for a meal or prayer during these forty days of Resurrection. The Risen Lord is truly in our midst. The ten days until Pentecost could be marked with a daily gathering for special prayer with Mary and the Apostles disposing us to receive more fully the Spirit who will guide us through the days ahead. A sharing of the Sunday readings at supper on Saturday or Sunday could help the household move with the whole people of God through the weeks of summer and fall so that the sense of participation in bringing about the ultimate victory and reign with Christ will be heightened. The liturgical year is our year, our life, but we share in its fruit and its hope only to the extent we do make it ours and enter into its movement.

The daughters and sons of Saint Benedict are characterized by their zeal for the Work of God, for the celebration of the liturgy as the summing up and expression of the glorification of God that ascends from the whole of creation. Benedict keeps his monks close to the movement of the creation. His horarium flows with the hours of the day and the seasons of the year. Nuns and monks know the longer quieter hours of watching of the winter and the more active days of seed time and harvest. They are priests of creation. A good ecology, a reverence for life are an important part of it. But this is the call of all the baptized. As I have said we are all baptized into Christ's priesthood, the priesthood of creation. Don't let artificial light and city streets keep you from noticing sunsets and sunrises, from experiencing the spring of new life and the harvest of fall. If you don't have a farm, at least have a window box or a few pots of earth. We are the priests of creation. We are the priests of a sinful human family. At this moment the prospects of history are bleak and threaten to become even more bleak. All the more reason why we have to live to the full, in liturgical mystery, the history of salvation. We still sin. Christ still saves. In the end *he will reign.* Whether we must first pass through a cataclysm, a nuclear holocaust or not—different ones interpret the Scriptures differently—in the end *he will reign.* And we with him. And even now, in the liturgy, we are welcome to experience already the ultimate triumph in the reign of Christ our King. Perhaps now more than ever before does zeal for the work of God need to characterize the Christian to bring healing and hope to a world so desperately in need of the presence of the saving Passion of Christ and his ultimate act of love.

And Our Work

S aint Benedict certainly held labor in high regard: "When they live by the labor of their hands, like our Fathers and the Apostles, then they are truly monks." He could have chosen yet an even more sublime model: the Lord Jesus himself. For the short time he spent on earth the greater part of it was spent as a laborer, planing wood and fitting it, delivering orders and bringing in supplies. Later he would choose largely laborers to form his chosen band, though "white collar" workers were not left out. Paul, that apostle come lately, though a well-educated rabbi, prided himself on living by the labor of his own hands. The Fathers of Egypt were known to weave and unweave baskets to keep busy but, more practically, they also raised grain and sent it down the river to the poor of Alexandria.

Work is the primal penance imposed upon us by God: By the sweat of your brow you will earn your bread. His Son and his Son's followers have embraced this penance. It is a basic part of Christian asceticism, far more healthy and productive than any of the extras: hairshirts, disciplines (little cord whips used to beat oneself) or whatever else. The Father of

Bakery
Holy Cross Abbey
Berryville, VA

Western nuns and monks had nothing to say concerning the feats of the desert ascetics. In fact, he does not even develop the idea of work as penance. He is more concerned about his monks being kept busy so that they will not be the idle playthings of the evil one: Idleness is the enemy of the soul. Indeed, Saint Benedict, far from emphasizing the penitential aspect of work, shows himself a solicitous father. The weak are to have work to keep them busy but not such that would overwhelm them or drive them away. They are to have help so they may serve without distress. The monks are to be suitably wined and dined so they can work without grumbling. Indeed all work is to be done in moderation with consideration for the fainthearted. This hardly sounds like a penitential regime.

Saint Benedict's thrust lies in another direction. He does not actually develop his theology of work. He sends his disciples to Saint Basil for the deeper aspects of monastic spirituality. The great monastic Father of the Eastern Christians does write at length about this aspect of the monk's life.

Saint Basil's teaching on work is contained substantially in six chapters or the responses to six questions in his longer Rules. The first, Question 37, lays a solid theological foundation for his teaching on work. Much of it is applicable to all Christians, based as it is on the teaching of Sacred Scripture, placing work squarely in the context of a life of prayer.

The Saint's exegesis is sometimes surprising. His

main base is no particular text but the example of Christ. And that is as it should be for all who call themselves Christians, followers of Christ, and for the monks who are to find their primary spiritual father in the Father of the World to Come. Saint Paul is also a model, he who so forcefully proclaimed himself a spiritual father, because he is such a whole-hearted follower and imitator of Christ our Master.

Although Saint Basil does not neglect the important ascetical and penitential aspects of work—for him it involves struggle and grave endeavor, fostering the growth of patience and bringing the body into subjection—he nowhere in these chapters alludes to the primal text of Genesis: "By the sweat of your brow you will earn your bread." Rather, when he comes to speak of the aims and dispositions that should motivate the Christian monk in his labor, he downplays this role of earning one's own bread. Paul's classic text: ". . . working, they would eat their own bread," Basil insists, is directed toward the unruly. And in their case, their work for their own food is better than their general uselessness; at least they will not be a burden to others. The emphasis for this very community-minded Father is on the other. Paul prided himself on his own manual labor in that it freed him from being a burden to others. We are not to seek our own—"Be not solicitous for your life, what you shall eat, nor for your body, what you shall put on." The Christian works that he might have to give others, for the other is Christ. To trust in one's own work, or even in that of others of the brotherhood, is forbidden. Basil does not forbid monks from working to support themselves—he expects them to do it—but in their labors they are to seek to earn, not to make themselves comfortable, but to have something to help others. All selfishness and self-reliance is set aside. Depending on the Lord, the Christian works for him, in himself and in those with whom he identifies himself.

The Apostle's command "to pray without ceasing" is not to be used as an excuse for holding back from work. Monks, Christians are to pray while they work. As he expands on this, Saint Basil gives us some precious teaching.

First of all the Saint is very realistic. Sometimes we can pray and recite psalms while we work. Saint Pachomius, with whom Basil was surely familiar, made elaborate provisions for this. But Basil recognizes that sometimes this is not possible or it is not conducive to edification. It would be forced. In such circumstances we can at least seek to praise God in our hearts with psalms, hymns and spiritual canticles. Yet he goes farther. Conscious of how God is at every moment truly present in his creative love, bringing forth all that is, Basil notes that we can praise God by being in touch with the reality that it is God who is at each moment of our labor (as I write this chapter and as you read it) giving to our hands and all our faculties the strength to do the task and to our minds the knowledge and insight to inspire and direct it. Furthermore, it is he, present and active, who is providing the materials—keeping them in being in his creative love—that we are using: both the instruments (this word processor, my brother's chisel or shovel or tractor) and the matter (my paper, his wood or metal or grain). The fully responsible use of these, of our own activity and the ordination of it all to "the good pleasure of God," is the practical way in which we do pray constantly.

Obedience to the Lord, a constant attentiveness to his presence in all, in the full responsiveness of obedience, this is fundamental in Saint Basil's attitude toward work. Given this, the other attitudes he would have enliven our work are not surprising. We are to go to work with enthusiasm, a ready zeal, and yet give each task careful attention. We are to strive to work blamelessly because we know that the true, ever-present overseer is none other than the Lord himself.

Saint Benedict only hints at the richness of Saint Basil's theology in a very telling sentence: all the tools and goods of the monastery are to be looked upon as the vessels of the altar. In our labor we are celebrating a liturgy, the liturgy of creation. Through the sentiments of his mind and heart the things he works with are lifted up to glorify God in a way that is worthy of him. They enter into a free, rational and living worship. The monk as he works is to be conscious of his duty to cooperate with the Divine creative energies in moving the creation along toward its goal not only through inducing new material and spiritual forms but in ordering all to the glory of God.

All Christians are called to this. Each task no matter how humdrum, be it mowing the lawn or keeping the accounts or any other work, moves the creative project forward. If it is done with love, it brings it to consummation.

We are called to constant watchfulness and prayer: "Pray without ceasing." Work has been seen by some as the greatest obstacle to this. Some even used this as an excuse not to work. Saint Pachomius, the Father of Cenobitism, sought to remedy this by assigning many prayers to be recited while the monks carried out their tasks. There was a whole liturgy for the bakers, prayers for each step in the making of the bread. This was carried to excess with the Cluniac monks. Saint Peter Damian tells rather humorously how the monks said so many prayers going to and coming from work and preparing for work that there was scarcely any time for the actual work. As we have seen, Saint Basil took another tack, a more intrinsic one. He would have us be aware that what we are working with is an immediate gift from God to us, that the tools we are using are his gift, and indeed the very energies with which we labor, that flow through our minds and bodies, are his immediate activity in us. Thus all work is prayer, an immediate communion with God in his creative activity. It is saying in deed, which speaks louder and more convincingly than word: "Thy will be done."

Thus we see there are many aspects to labor: it is penance, an opportunity to make reparation for our sins; it frees us from idleness; it offers us an opportunity to serve others either immediately or through giving alms; it is prayer; it is collaborating with God in bringing his creation to its consummation; it is a call to glorify the Maker of All. Undoubtedly some forms of work seem to fall more into one aspect and others into another. Our own attitudes will incline us habitually or occasionally to emphasize one or another of these dimensions. The important thing is not to fall into a shallow or materialistic outlook where work is just work or takes on only its own materialistic ends. Such work is not worthy of those who are made in the image of God Himself. We do have to make a living. Jobs do need to get done. Works of art have their own intrinsic beauty. Ordering our work to higher goals will not detract from all this. It will only enhance these ends, incorporate them into the overall thrust of life and augment our dedication to accomplishing them, doing the work well to the best of our ability.

We make fruitcake in my monastery. We do it to help support ourselves and it does that well enough. We seek to make the finest fruitcake on the market, and many do say that Assumption Abbey fruitcake is the best. In taking in hand the fine ingredients we use, fruit of the earth and labor of human hands, through a labor of love we give them the opportunity to serve people and glorify God in a new higher way. We are happy that we can bring additional sweetness to the lives of many through our product. It is our joy to be able to send some cases of them to a nearby city to give joy and nourishment to our less fortunate sisters and brothers. Sometimes, especially as the hot humid summer days come along or the machinery begins to break down, work in our bakery can be very penitential. But in the end, we do all that we do there because we love God and want to glorify him in Christ, our Lord—the same ultimate reason why I write books, Brother Tom mows lawns, Father Ted plays the organ, Father Richard works with the computer and Father David welcomes guests.

You have your work. It will be more meaningful for you, whatever it may be, if you take all the opportunities it affords to serve and give joy to others; if you reverence things you work with and are conscious that your working with them gives them an opportunity to express themselves at a higher level through your activity and love; if you share some of the fruit of your labor with those less fortunate; if you do all for the love and glory of God, knowing then that your work is part of the transformation of the whole of creation, including especially yourself.

A good way to begin moving in this direction is to begin each day with a morning offering. Pray:

Jesus, I offer you all my prayer, work, joy and sufferings of this day for all the intentions of your Sacred Heart, in union with the holy sacrifice of the Mass throughout the world, in reparation for my sins and for the intentions. . . .

Then, as the day progresses, renew this offering as often as you can.

I do not want to write about work and not write about Sabbath rest. The Lord worked powerfully for six days. He saw that his work was good, very good. And he rested. It is true, the Father works until now. The creation is ever going on. Monks celebrate the Work of God every day. There are tasks that must be taken care of every day. But the Genesis account of the Creator's labor and all the details of the Sabbath laws are God's way of making us aware of a profound human need: to stop, step back from our work and take perspective. It is very true that if we do not do this, very quickly the motives which make our work worthy of us as human persons, Christians, sharers of the Divine Nature, are lost and work itself begins to own us and set its own goals. There is much more to the Sabbath rest than getting perspective on our work. But this is an important aspect of it. If we do find that our work is encroaching on the time we should be taking for family, leisure, friendship and prayer, it is time to take warning. In these days when technology has so altered the natural rhythm of human life, it is unfortunately not possible for everyone to enjoy the rhythm of a Sabbath week. It is a value not to be readily given up. But if you are forced to, you will want to establish a rhythm in your life where periodically, according to your need, you do step back from your regular work and take the space necessary to keep it in perspective.

Sabbath space should not be quickly filled with other albeit different activities. Some diversification of activity can be recreative. But we do need space to be, to let our true selves with our deeper aspirations come to the surface. It is in such leisure we gain perspective and see if our work is what we truly want it to be. Does it have the place in our life we want it to have? Is it moving in the direction we want it to move? And how about our family life, our leisure, our friendships: do we get what we want to get out of them? Do we really do what we want to do? It takes some real space and quiet to get sufficiently in touch with ourselves to answer these questions to our full satisfaction. Perhaps we avoid leisure and keep on filling our time because we are afraid of negative answers and being confronted with the meaninglessness of much of what we are doing or the ultimate insufficiency of our motivation. If you do not find in your life a good balance of work and Sabbath, then something needs to be examined.

When I show guests through the monastery occasionally on a Sunday, they are struck by the stillness. They ask if anyone is really at home. The monks love their Sabbath rest. At the same time the guests will comment on how clean everything is, how well the lawns are manicured, how beautiful the vesture is, how good our fruitcakes are, how peaceful is the whole climate of the monastery. In our rest, the fruit of our labor is present to be enjoyed. That is the way it should be. If your work is relentless, if there are not periodically spaces of leisure where you and your loved ones can enjoy together the fruit of your labor, then something is wrong. We should do all God wants us to do. If we are not finding due Sabbath we are perhaps doing more than he wants, doing things he wants others to do or wants to take care of himself.

As I write this, I am painfully aware that at this time there are all too many who cannot find work or work that will adequately remunerate them so they can establish a balance in their lives. It would be difficult to overestimate how dehumanizing this can be, how much it can undermine a person's humanity and participative divinity. We are meant to be participating with the Creator in the ongoing work of bringing the creation to completion. What can I say to these sisters and brothers? To those of us who are better off, I think each of us according to our proper vocation should do all we can economically, socially, politically and through prayer to remedy this situation. To the unemployed and the underemployed, I hesitate to say anything—words come cheap. But faith does come through hearing. Behind all the inhumanity of people and their plain bungling, there abides a loving and provident God. Trust in him can be the source which will enable you to keep going, keep trying, working out your salvation maybe not with the sweat of your brow but the tears of your heart. God help you, and us all.

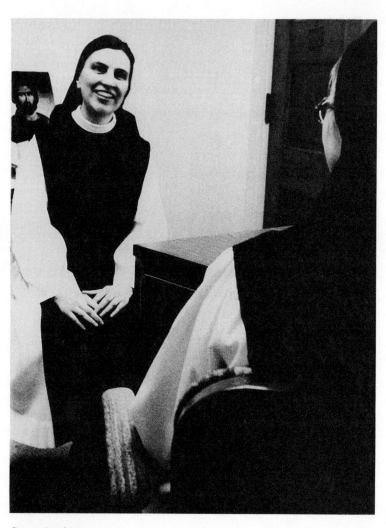

Consultation
Mount Saint Mary's Abbey
Wrentham, MA

The Way of Obedience

*T*here is a classical story that comes from the desert tradition. It is ascribed to many different Fathers. In one version it goes something like this:

It was said of Abba John the Dwarf that he withdrew and lived in the desert at Scete with an old man of Thebes. His abba, taking a piece of dry wood, planted it and said to him, "Water it every day with a bottle of water until it bears fruit." At the end of three years the wood came to life and bore fruit. Then the old man took some of the fruit and carried it to the church, saying to the brethren, "Take and eat the fruit of obedience."

Obedience was held in highest esteem by these desert Fathers and pushed sometimes to extremes:

One of the inhabitants of the Thebaid came to see Abba Siseos one day because he wanted to become a monk. The old man asked him if he had any relations in the world. He replied, "I have a son." The old man said, "Go and throw him in the river, then you can become a monk." As he went to throw him in, the old man sent a brother in haste to prevent him, "Stop what you are doing." But the other replied, "The abba told me to throw him in." So the other said, "But afterwards he said not to throw him in." So he left his son and went to find the old man and became a monk, tested by obedience.

There is, of course, something of a biblical precedent for this test, but it is a bit frightening when men act as God. These men had a simplicity that dared such things, for they were of the race of Abraham, men of obedience, and it was for them the great virtue.

Four monks of Scitis came one day to see the great abba, Pambo. Each one spoke of the virtue of his neighbor. The first fasted a great deal; the second embraced great poverty; the third had acquired great charity; and the fourth they said had lived twenty-two years in obedience to a senior. Abba Pambo said, "I tell you the virtue of the last is the greatest. Each of the others has acquired the virtue he sought. But the last one, restraining his own will, does the will of another. Now it is of such men that the martyrs are made, if they persevere to the end."

Abba Rufus expatiated on this at greater length:

He who remains sitting at the feet of his spiritual father receives a greater reward than he who lives alone in the desert. One of the Fathers said, "I have seen four orders in heaven: in the first order is the sick man who gives thanks to God; in the second, the man who observes hospitality and for that reason gets up to serve; in the third, the man who crosses the desert without seeing anyone; in the fourth, the man who obeys his Father and remains in submission to him for the Lord's sake. The one who was living in submission was wearing a chain of gold and a shield and had greater glory than the others. I said to him who was guiding me, "Why does the one who is least have more glory that the others?" He answered me, "He who practices hospitality acts according to his own will; he who lives in the desert goes the way of his own free will; but the last one possesses obedience. Having abandoned all his desires, he depends on God and his own Father; it is because of this that he has received more glory than the others." See, my child, how good obedience is when it is undertaken for the Lord. You have partly understood the elements of this virtue, my children. O obedience, salvation of the faithful! O obedience, mother of all the virtues! O obedience, discloser of the kingdom! O obedience, opening the heavens and making men to ascend there from earth! O obedience, food of all the saints, whose milk they have sucked, through you they have become perfect! O obedience, companion of the angels!

Amma Syncletica (there were desert mothers, too!) was more succinct: "Obedience is preferable to asceticism." Indeed, Abba Antony the Great said, "Obedience with abstinence gives me power over wild beasts" (the beasts being the strong passions that rage within us). Abba Hyperachios indicates why obedience is held in such high regard:

Obedience is the best ornament of the monk. He who has acquired it will be heard by God and he will stand beside the Crucified with confidence for the Crucified Lord became obedient unto death.

In a word (according to Abba Isadore), "In obeying the truth, one surpasses everything else, for such a one is the image and likeness of God."

Saint Benedict is then very much in line with the tradition when he begins his *Rule for Monasteries:*

> Listen carefully, my son, to the master's instructions and attend to them with the ear of your heart. This is advice from a father who loves you; welcome it and faithfully put it in practice. The labor of obedience will bring you back to him from whom you had drifted through the sloth of disobedience.

In every human grouping, even if it be only two or three, someone has to be empowered, at least transiently, to make the decisions, or the group will often be paralyzed. The richness of human personalities, the multiplicity of possibilities, make consensus an elusive goal, often difficult if not impossible to attain. And life must go on. So consensus expresses itself in the willingness to choose or accept and obey a leader.

But the obedience of which the Fathers speak is not primarily the functional obedience required by organization, however important this may be to the good order of the monastery and monastic community. The Fathers are concerned with deeper values.

By innate dignity, all human persons are essentially equal. It is below our dignity to obey any other human person simply as a human person. If we do obey a superior or boss in a community or organization, it is because we freely choose to cooperate with the group in attaining its goals. A good of obedience is here—we cooperate as equals with different roles —but not *the good* of obedience.

One alone is to be obeyed ultimately: God in his guiding Spirit. "Eye has not seen, nor ear heard, nor has it entered into the heart of the human person what God has prepared for those who love him, but the Holy Spirit makes it known to us." We want to know the will of God, and fully conform ourselves to it. This is the only way to complete human happiness. God made us to be happy with him.

Recently I received one of those new watches with a number of buttons on each side. When I push one it lights up, when I push another I get the date, a third will turn it into a stopwatch, and so on. Fortunately for me there was a booklet with the watch which explained it all: if I push the third button twice I reset the alarm, and so forth. If I cavalierly threw away the booklet, I might have eventually figured it all out—*might*—and after a long time. The human person with his infinite potential is the most enriched being in God's creation. The Lord has given us means of knowing how to attain our purpose, how to function well and be happy. This involves obeying him in his Scriptures (his rule book) and his Church (the guide who helps us interpret the rule book). All too many of us cavalierly throw the rule book away or leave it unread and ignore his Church. Even those of us who do accept these find it difficult to be constant in our response to them. We have lots of ideas of our own.

So the nun and monk enter a "school of the Lord's service." By committing ourselves to obey a superior and making such obedience a part of our daily practice, we hope to learn how better to obey the Lord. More practiced in setting aside our own will, we can more readily conform to the Divine will.

But there is more to monastic obedience than this. It is not always easy to discern the will of God in all the details of life. By entrusting our way to a *pneumaticos*, a spirit-filled abba or amma, we can benefit by the discernment of one who is more under the influence of the Spirit than ourselves. In the later institutionalization of the monastic orders there has been added to this the gift which Christ gave to his Church to guide: "He who hears you, hears me." Nevertheless, Saint Bernard of Clairvaux constantly exhorted his monks to pray most earnestly that he would be guided by the Spirit in serving them. It is the faith of the disciples which guarantees that God will not let them down in the guidance they receive from their superiors.

One of the benefits of this obedience is freedom. The monk walking in the way of obedience is freed from having to devote time and energy to discerning God's will in so many of the details of life. He can simply do what he is told and walk with God. This could, of course, be a disguise for laziness or undue dependency. It is only the mature who can truly obey, like Christ. The dependent go with the flow for less than fully human reasons, rather than seek maturely to embrace the will of God. The immature struggling for a sense of self cannot obey for they fear that in submitting themselves to another they will lose themselves. Mature persons can submit themselves freely to another without fear of losing themselves. They rather see obedience as the way to more surely attain what they want.

There is yet another important dimension to obedience beyond the ascetical. In vowing obedience as nuns and monks do we place ourselves wholly at the disposal of the Church: the local Church (our community) and the Church universal. We become gifts. We are to lay down our lives for our brethren and friends. In our lifetime commitment we seek to be one with our Master who was obedient unto death. Obedience is the fulfillment of discipleship. But for the Christian it is more. We have been baptized into Christ, made profoundly one with him. To be fully who we are, we want, like him, to seek always to do the things that please the Father. This is the summit of Christian obedience. "He who loves me, keeps my commandments." It is the expression of love that wants to be wholly one with the Beloved. If as nuns or monks we open ourselves to allowing even the least details of our lives to be regulated, it is because we want to be totally conformed to the will of God, our Beloved. I exist not to do my own will but the will of him who created me. Thy will be done.

The average lay person has plenty of opportunities to obey. There are red lights and the stop signs, speed limits and traffic cops; there are laws of all sorts. We can obey out of fear of the consequences or out of consideration of others and good order. But we can go beyond this and see even in these details of life an opportunity to come into harmony with the will of God, to express our love for him. Saint Paul reminds us: All government comes from God. And Saint Peter: For the sake of the Lord, accept the authority of every social institution. . . . God wants you to be good citizens. There is also the obedience due to the Church, which touches so many details of life if we are listening. There is the obedience that makes things flow smoothly and efficiently at the office or shop. There is obedience within the home.

True obedience doesn't involve just doing what we are told. There can be a call to blind obedience but there is great danger that such obedience will be infantile. True obedience involves a responsibility to help the superior or leader in discernment. We do not want blind authority. We want to help authority to discern. The superior, too, must be a person of obedience, listening to what God is saying through those he is called to lead—as Saint Benedict says: The Spirit sometimes speaks through the juniors—and we must be obedient to that.

Saint Benedict has a most curious chapter in his Rule: What we are to do if the superior assigns an impossible task. The Holy Father says the monk is to choose an appropriate time and patiently explain his inability to his superior. But if the superior insists, he must in love obey. In so doing we sometimes find our judgment was off, influenced by our passions perhaps. Or we find God coming to our assistance and supplying for our limitations. However, in the event we find the task is actually impossible, God teaches us, our superiors and others through our failures.

If there is one instance in the Rule when the loving and benign Father of Monte Cassino speaks with vehemence it is when he condemns the vice of murmuring. As we perceive the good of obedience we can see why he does. If the heart of obedience is a quest to be a complete "yes" to God in love, murmuring is diametrically opposed to this. Obedience with murmuring is a charade. It is obedience motivated by some intention not worthy of the human person. It is to miss the whole point of obedience.

Another precious school of obedience a lay person can choose is that found in a relationship with a spiritual mother or father. In the Eastern or Byzantine Christian tradition this practice remains fully alive. The renewal of the Sacrament of Reconciliation in our Western tradition is a good step in this direction. The reconciliation room offers the opportunity to sit down and have a good, sincere, open talk on a regular basis with a spiritual father. If we come with faith and confidence we can depend on God to speak to us through him. Oftentimes it is only when we talk something out openly and frankly with another person that we hear clearly what the Holy Spirit—the only true director of the human spirit—is saying within us.

Saul of Tarsus was riding high as he approached the gates of Damascus. He thought he knew well the will of God. He was sincerely seeking to carry it out. God would not let such sincerity down. He threw Saul down from his high horse and spoke to him. But he did not will to reveal all to him directly: "Go to Ananias." God can and does speak to us directly in the depths of our heart, but his ordinary way of making his will known to us is through the Church, through a spiritual mother or father. If we truly want to be guided by the creative will of God which is wholly ordered to the glory of God in our happiness and fulfillment, we will want to use all the means we can to assure that we are clearly hearing it and empowered to live it.

The good of obedience, which Saint Benedict and the whole Christian tradition so highly extols, is perhaps a value little appreciated in our times. A false sense of the democratic spirit does not appreciate it. But if we reflect on its values we soon become eager to embrace it. This is not to deny that it is a difficult path to follow. Our Master sweated blood and begged to be let off even though obedience was the most profound aspiration of his life and was the way that would lead to glory:

Let this mind be in you which is in Christ
Jesus. Although he is equal to God in all
things he emptied himself becoming obedient, obedient unto death. Wherefore God
has highly exalted him and has given him a
name above every other name.

Obedience pertains to the essence of Christian life.

And of Joy

We all tend to have our favorite Gospel. For the contemplative it is often Saint John's. The transcendence of his Prologue and the deep sharing of the Sacred Heart at the Last Supper speak deeply to my heart. Some are drawn more by the conciseness and actuality of Saint Mark. I have appreciated Saint Matthew's sense of tradition and fulfillment, his Jewishness. Saint Luke is the ladies' man. Women loom large in his account of salvation history. But it is his joy, especially in the first chapter, that has particularly attracted me to him. The angels sing, the shepherds rejoice. Mary proclaims her Magnificat and old Zachariah his Benedictus. And Simeon closes his long life in fulfilled song.

Saint Luke undoubtedly belongs to a tradition, a vein of Judaism which, despite the awesomeness of the God of Sinai, has been able to celebrate his holiness in joy, dancing in spirit with Miriam on the banks of the Red Sea and with David before the Ark. Its joy reaches down to our times in the Hasidim who have brought their heritage through the pogroms of Eastern Europe to Brooklyn Heights.

Cook and assistant
Assumption Abbey
Ava, MO

Monika Hellwig described the spiritual outlook of the Hasidim:

> The objective of hasidic spirituality is to become aware of God and united to God everywhere and in all things with sustained passionate and joyful self-abandonment. For the Hasidim the presence of God everywhere and in all things was understood literally. Therefore, intimate union with God was to be sought not only in seclusion but in the everyday life of the community.

As I read these lines I thought how well they also describe the monastic spirituality of the Cistercians. Happiness consists in knowing what you want and knowing you have it or on the way to getting it. Those who truly seek God, who want God and have the insight of faith and the gifts of the Holy Spirit to perceive his real presence in everyone and everything, always have what they want. They know that the whole world is the place of God, that all is sacred. They are always happy. Their lives express that joy which is a fruit of the Holy Spirit.

The monk who embraces the primal penance of men: "By the sweat of your brow you will earn your bread," and seeks to support himself by daily manual labor, cannot draw a line between his work and his religious practices. He must seek to overcome any separation of the sacred and the profane and be open to the encounter with God in all. Guerric, the abbot of Igny, a chosen disciple of Bernard of Clairvaux, speaking to his monks one Easter morning brought this out. He was commenting on the Gospel passage where the pious women had gone to Jesus' tomb to anoint him and found it empty. As they returned along the garden path they came upon him. Guerric reminded his monks how it sometimes happened that they seemed to seek the Lord in vain as they pursued their sacred reading, went to the Office and prayed at the tomb of the altar. But as they went off down the path toward their appointed labor—lo! there was the Lord.

If the monk goes apart from the world, it is to go to the heart of the world. If he is a fringe person it is not because he is on the outer fringe but the inner fringe. His vocation is one of redeeming the world by a recovery of the integrity of Eden, where in communion and union all the divorce between the sacred and the secular is healed. The community of love, embracing all creation, standing in God—this is the ideal of the monastic school of love. Daily practice and a lively hope bring the joy of knowing it as an attainable object that is actually being attained.

Singlemindedness which comes from inner devotion and purity of intention sees only one goal in life. People who truly seek God see all "as it were under a single ray of light." "Whether you eat or drink or whatever else you do, do all for the glory of God." All, natural objectives, human activities, social structures, all take on a power and unity, all contribute to what the monk seeks and, therefore, to his joy.

The humility of the Gospels and of the Rule of Saint Benedict—true humility—is not a demeaning of self, comparing self with others, striving to evaluate or devaluate self. No. It is rather a realistic grasp and acceptance of the reality that one is part of the whole, a member of the community, of Christ. The wonder of one's being is still part of something, someone so very much greater. And there is a joy that transcends self in this realization.

It can readily be seen how these two virtues complement each other. The singlemindedness, the devotion keeps us from turning in on ourselves. And our freedom from self-absorption enables us to be wholly turned toward the Lord.

The work of service or the service of work is the responsive gift of self in obedience to reality. It involves the work of worship, the response to the transcendent reality of God as well as the work of service, the response to the needs of our sisters and brothers, the needs of a creation that is groaning and in travail as it strives for the fullness of redemption. Whether the service be sublime or most humble, it is all one, seeking to bring about the ascension of all to God in integral harmony.

Complementary to this daily and sometimes laborious service is the experience of God, the going out of self, the "taste and see how good God is," that engenders a joy that seems to belong to another realm. The peak moments of ecstasy will be few and brief, but the memory of them abides, renewed each time we gather to celebrate the work of God. And something deep within us says that all the strivings of life are worthwhile because of them. The joy of these moments continues to flow as a deep, abiding current in our lives, to be called forth through devotion and service.

There are spontaneous eruptions of joy in the lives of all of us. But such an abiding state of joy does not just happen. It has to be cultivated. It is an option. If I may descend to a very prosaic simile, I often say that the whole world is made up of two kinds of people: those who look at the doughnut and those who look at the hole. Some prefer to dwell on the emptiness of life, the lacks, what is missing, not realizing that there cannot be a lack, something missing, a hole, if there is not a context, a fullness from which it is missing. We can choose to dwell on the fullness, on being rather than on the lack of being. We can see the glass is half full rather than half empty.

I think it is sadly true that in general people are programmed for suffering more than for joy. We seem almost to enjoy talking about our miseries and dwelling on them. There are no doubt abundant causes for sorrow, concern and grief. But where sin abounds—and all its effects—grace abounds yet more. We can opt to keep our eyes on the presence and activity of grace in our own lives and in the lives of others and accentuate this with all its hope.

Reprogramming may call for effort, a real program on our part. We can begin by smiling more. Every human being rates a smile and infinitely more. And the first person we might smile at each day is the one we greet in the bathroom mirror. We can make an effort to make pleasant and complimentary comments as often as possible. We all like to be told how good we look. Our smile and compliment will oftentimes evoke a similar response, reinforcing our own new direction. We can make a practice of letting go of unnecessary negative thoughts and feelings and cultivate joyful, positive ones. We can take time out to reflect on each person who holds a place in our lives, noticing all the good in each—and they are many, for each is the image of God—then share this with the person involved and others. Again, one of these persons should be that special person called "me." As an exercise we can think of the worst thing that might possibly happen, and then try to see all the positive things that might flow from it. For example, we might think of ourselves getting hit by a car and landing in the hospital. Positively, it might give us time to do some things we have been wanting to do: reading, writing, praying, painting. We will get a good rest. The insurance company may be good to us and we can make a trip we have been wanting. We might make new friends. Old friends will come and spend time with us. We will get our picture in the newspaper and on television. We will get a new car, and so forth. We can spend more time meditating on the positive aspects of our faith: God's great love for us, Christ's saving grace, the heaven that awaits us, and thank God for all this. Thanksgiving is a source of double joy. And sharing all these reflections with another, a friend, will multiply our joy.

An important part of our program will be review and evaluation. We might each evening at our Compline prayer reflect for a moment on the particular practice we are presently concentrating on: How many times today did I smile? How many times did I fail to smile when I could have? How many compliments did I give today? How many opportunities to say a complimentary word did I miss? How often did I harbor unnecessary negative thoughts and feelings? How often did I cultivate and express positive ones? On our monthly retreat day we will want to evaluate our program and its degree of success in reprogramming us for joy. It will probably have to be adapted as we make progress in the direction we want to go.

One would wonder why all do not choose to dwell on the fullness. But a little reflection quickly gives some indications. Such fullness demands a response; it calls forth that inner devotion. It makes us realize our own relative position, the attitude of true humility. It calls for service. There is a cost. But when the cost is paid, it will lead us to joy and ecstasy. Some would rather not pay the price. Nothingness, the hole, makes no demands. We can easily feel superior to a hole. Keeping an eye on the lacks in others enables us to live more comfortably with our own—

or so we think, as long as we are coming out of comparative thinking. We can find lots of "reasons" for looking at the holes in life: One must be realistic, practical, prudent, etc. And there is some truth in these reasons. But if we don't see the holes in the context of the fullness, these reasons no longer have any validity. And they do deprive us of so much of the joy of life. To have the courage to look at the fullness of reality and let it call us forth is the way to ever greater joy.

God our beloved Father has made a tremendously beautiful universe, and he has made it all for us, for our happiness. We have sadly ignored and countered his plan in many, many ways. His healing grace is at work. If it is initially painful to face the wonder of his love and be convicted of our own unresponsiveness, his mercy is not slow in responding to our misery. Even the past misery becomes a source of joy as we experience the soothing of his healing love.

I remember one of the answers I learned by rote back in Our Lady of Angels grade school: God made me to know, love and serve him in this world and to be happy with him in the next. I think that catechism answer conveys a real heresy, one that has perhaps done more to undermine Christian life than we can estimate. The implication that God's plan reserves happiness for heaven is enough to cause us at least to question his love if not actually to turn against such a Father. God made us to be happy with him not only in the next life but here and now. Saint Paul reminds us that the fruits of a life in the Spirit are love and joy. Surely there will be sorrows on the journey. The true lover is ever more sensitive to the suffering of others and the injustices of our society. But deep within, a person in tune with God experiences a constant joy. This is the prerogative of the Christian, the one baptized into Christ, who has in baptism received the Spirit as a gift. The important thing is that we give ourselves time and space to enjoy the friendship of God, to experience his love and his care, to let the whole creation reveal to us his love. Let's keep our eyes on the doughnut and the hole will fill with sweetness—and we shall have a jelly doughnut!

The Fasting Attitude:
A Christian Approach
to Reality

*S*aint Benedict has been reputed for his moderation, but the regime he spells out for his monks with regard to fasting sounds anything but moderate to many of us moderns: one meal a day most of the year and that in late afternoon or evening. For the time and the place, though, and in comparison with the feats of his monastic forebears, he was moderate indeed.

> At one time Abba Agathon had two disciples, each leading the anchoritic life according to his own measure. One day he asked the first: "How do you live in the cell?" He replied: "I fast until evening, then I eat two hard biscuits." He said to him, "Your way of life is good, not overburdened with too much asceticism." Then he asked the other one, "And you, how do you live?" He re-

Refectory
Saint Joseph's Abbey
Spencer, MA

plied: "I fast for two days and then I eat two hard biscuits."

Benedict's Rule, then, of one meal a day was no departure from the tradition. But the temperate legislator did temper its rigor. There was, of course, no fast during the holy Paschal season nor on the day of Resurrection, Sunday. Such a fast would be heretical. The Bridegroom is with his Church. It is no time for fasting but only for a wedding feast. With Pentecost, the fast can return, but Benedict would limit it to two days a week and even these would be dispensed with if the heat or the summer work would make a fast too burdensome.

When the monastic fast was resumed in the fall, Abba Benedict was loath to prescribe a precise regime: "Each has his own proper gift from God: one this, one that. And therefore it is with some diffidence that a measure of food is established by us." At all meals there are to be two cooked portions so that if a monk cannot eat of the one he at least has the other. If the work is heavy, more is to be given. If the garden offers it, salad and fruit are added. Even though tradition proscribed wine for monks, Benedict bends to the custom of his time and country and allows a healthy portion. He warns only against overdoing things and invites the monks to do more on their own, especially during Lent.

Benedict's true disciples have always held fasting in high regard. Mitigations have come in through the centuries. When they are in response to real need they are fully legitimate, for the wise legislator always left it to the discretion of the local abbot to adapt the Rule to the circumstances. But "frugality should be the rule on all occasions"—a frugality that left the tummy grumbling at times. As one of Benedict's later disciples, the twelfth-century Cistercian Isaac of Stella, put it: "The man who eats whenever he is hungry doesn't have any idea what a fast is. The virtue and merit of fasting begin only when one is hungry." Fasting really counts only when one hungers, and the longer this endures, the more the fast counts.

This is Isaac's brief word on fasting, at least on physical fasting. But he immediately goes on to say: "There is another more sacred and higher type of fasting." Fasting is a life attitude and its significance lies in establishing that kind of relationship with the creation that serves the main thrust of Christian life —the desire for union and fullness of life in Christ. In his chapter on Lent, Saint Benedict writes:

> . . . each one may offer up to God in the joy of the Holy Spirit something over and above the measure appointed him: that is, let him deny his body in food, in drink, in sleep, in superfluous talking and mirth, and withal

long for the holy feast of Easter with the joy
of holy desire.

A physical emptiness and hunger supports a spiritual
hunger, a hunger for God.

Fasting is an attitude of life marked by joy because it is a stance toward Creator and creation that is
dictated by the desires of love. Such an attitude is
wholly foreign to anything picayune, though nothing
is so small as not to merit its due appreciation and
place. It is not at all tied up with little rules and regula-
tions, yet it does not fail to appreciate the human
imperative of incarnation and communal order and
expression. There is a time, and there needs to be a
time, when the Christian community, whether it be
the cellular local community or one of larger compo-
nents of the worldwide Christian body, together af-
firms in a coordinated and significant way (by a sign
that speaks) its adhesion to the values inherent in
fasting. Every community and every household
needs to be aware of this to incarnate our values in
ways that witness to our membership in the ecclesial
community and allow for a healthy experience of our
basic unity.

As Christians, one of the basic reasons for
adopting a fasting attitude toward life and the source
of our perceiving its values is our devotion to Christ
and our adherence to him as Master. We want to be

Christ's disciples and follow in his way, the way to fuller, risen life.

Christ's forty days in the desert, with its almost total fast from the presence and use of the things of creation, is very striking. It underlines the value of an occasional radical withdrawal from the use and enjoyment of things and even from the society of friends, especially as a preparation for a significant undertaking.

But Christ's whole life was marked with a certain sobriety in his use of things. As he tramped the roads on his life's mission he did not keep any comfortable nest to return to. "The Son of Man had not whereon to lay his head." He took things as he found them, made do (sleeping in the boat, for example, or at Peter's house), depended on his Father, shared with his friends, receiving their everyday care and benefactions and coming up with his own miraculous spread on occasion. He got along frugally, but there was time for the splurge of the Passover feast. And a party at Levi's or Simon's was not turned down.

Most basic was his attitude to his Father in all. How many times did he say, "I thank you, Father"? How many times did he raise his eyes to heaven to bless God!

Not only as loving disciples of Christ, desirous of having his mind and heart, but as beloved children of the Father, gratitude shown by appreciation must mark our response to creation. Has not each one of us, at one time or another, known the pain of ingratitude when we have seen our gift lying broken and dusty in the corner or have discovered something we had esteemed at a price now wantonly wasted by a thoughtless recipient? All that we have, all that we are, is the gracious gift of our Father. The realization of this is the basis for a true ecology. The gift in itself is precious. But how much more value is added to it by our love of the Giver and his love for us. How offensive to him is a wanton, wasteful or useless consumption or destruction of his precious gifts! Love for the Father inspires us to hold each bit of creation as precious and to use it with due care.

None of us is an "only child." Christ is the first-born of many brethren. We have a whole world of sisters and brothers and many more to come. The Father's gifts are meant for all of us, to provide for the needs of all and for the good pleasure and life enrichment of us all. We are bound to one another by our common needs. We all need to eat. We all need to drink. We all need to be clothed. All of us—not just some of us. The ages yet to come—not just this generation. So, with love, we take care. We gratefully use what we need. We enjoy what is present to us. We try to see that all have the joy of sharing with us in this banquet of creation. In this sharing our joy is multiplied. Only the glutton can enjoy gorging himself alone. Even the hermit finds joy in knowing that the bit he is using is a sharing from the common table of the human family. When we fast and know the pangs of hunger we are in compassionate communion with our desperately hungry sisters and brothers in the ghettos and Appalachias of our own country as well as in the blighted corners and expanses of the globe. Out of the emptiness of each of us as individuals comes a fullness for all of us together.

Such privation does not really impoverish us. It is not necessary for us to consume created goods or to grasp them in material possession in order to be aggrandized by them. No. In fact, greedy consumption or a grasping subjection only impoverishes creation and reduces its potential to enrich us. It is only when we truly reverence the created and allow its goodness to speak to us in its own right that it can most fully bestow on us its richness—its share of the divine goodness and beauty.

As the glutton gulps down his carrots, he gets his proteins, carbohydrates and calories and a passing feeling of being full, but it is all so passing—except the unwanted calories. But one who has a reverent attitude of grateful appreciation can well be filled with the wonder of the carrot and savor its unique flavor, texture, color, and odor—truly enjoy it and be nourished by it in spirit as well as body. The grasping possessor reduces all he grasps to the sole value that inspires his grasping—dollars and cents, power, prestige, sensual satisfaction. The reverent and grateful recipient lets each thing express to him all its own unique values of goodness and beauty as well as the overwhelming love of the Giver.

A fasting attitude multiplies the enrichment

while it minimizes the consumption. And it gives birth to freedom.

We are poor, needy creatures, ever hanging on the mercy of God and of our fellow-travelers on this planet Earth. Yet how many of our experienced needs are truly needs? How much is our bondage multiplied by pseudo needs—those "needs" that come from Madison Avenue brainwashing or our own enslavement to habit? How freeing can be an experience of radical fasting from food when it teaches us in our guts that we can indeed survive and survive quite well without three square meals a day and all those calories, proteins and carbohydrates. And along with this there is that expansion of spiritual horizons that arises in us when we enjoy a period of significant abstinence from food and drink.

We can learn the freedom of getting along with less clothing, less heat, less sound to fill our silences, less objects to fill our spaces, less diversions to fill our time. The little, when given a chance to blossom can express all its own proper reality, can with its beauty fill to overflowing all our capacities. Think of a traditional Japanese floral arrangement. Each speck of creation is not only the gift of the Father. It is a participation in his very being with all its beauty. This is the joy about which Saint Benedict is speaking.

As we grow in gratitude and appreciation we need less and less of creation, we are freer and freer to find in ourselves, and in the expansive little we already have, all that we want and need. This is why

105

the poor can be the happiest. They have the freedom to enjoy fully all they have. "Blessed are the poor for theirs is the kingdom of heaven." Those who possess more must expend more time and energy taking care of their many things, with the result they have not the time to enjoy any of them freely and fully. Somoza possessed a large portion of the land in Nicaragua, yet he was said to be terribly jealous of the poor and persecuted them because they seemed to enjoy his land more than he did. Such men lose their freedom and become the servants or even the slaves of what they are said to possess. They do not possess—they are possessed.

Indeed, we can all ask ourselves as we look around at the clutter in our own lives, great or little as it might be: Do I possess or am I possessed? Do I use or am I used? Is this what Paul was talking about when he said we should use this creation as if we used it not? To be able to use the good things of our Father's beneficence and enjoy them in such a way that we retain our ability to use them not, to get along without them—this is true freedom.

Fasting in our time has taken on some new social dimensions, most significantly through the example of Mahatma Gandhi. It always had social dimensions for monks. The Fathers of the Egyptian desert deprived themselves of food and sent boatloads of grain down the river to feed the poor of Alexandria. Through the ages, whatever remained over at the table of the monks was taken to the gate to be shared with the poor. Not long ago I saw this being done in an Indian monastery. Where this is not feasible, monks have held their special fast days, feasting on bread and water or a bowl of rice in solidarity with the world's hungry and sending a check for what the regular meal would have cost to someone who could immediately care for the needy like Food for the Poor. With Gandhi, fasting also became a means to underline a cause, to proclaim that the attainment of certain values has more meaning than life itself, that for such values it is worth laying down one's life.

Such a fast can unfortunately be easily and subtly diverted from proclamation to weapon, from nonviolence to violence. One of Gandhi's rules for public fasting was that it "cannot be resorted to against those who regard us as their enemy or on whose love we have not established a claim by dint of selfless service." Fasting as a proclamation is in accord with the monastic tradition. For surely the monk's fast did proclaim life at its maximum. The tradition never espoused a fast unto death; rather fasting seems to have fostered longevity in monasteries. Their fasts did affirm that for a follower of Christ there are values greater than physical well-being.

Perhaps not much needs to be said by way of practical suggestion for integrating fasting into one's life in the everyday world. The moderation of Saint Benedict is generally to be espoused. Times and seasons of more fasting are good when done with counsel. The saintly Legislator would have his monks get the abbot's approval for all their Lenten extras. Each, according to health and labors, will have to find his or her own measure. Christ's disciples do fast in the absence of the Bridegroom. A weekly fast day, whatever the measure be—a complete fast, a water fast, or simply depriving oneself of dessert—would seem to be a good general rule. Except of course during the Holy Easter season.

Fasting is a true human good. Many today are more aware of this and are trying to experience it more. Many are being drawn to its strongly evocative presence among the devotees of Eastern religions. For us, the disciples of Christ, the attitude of fasting and the living out of it has been elevated, divinized, made fraternal and filial in the example of our Divine Master. Should not our lives be joyfully illumined and shine forth with this, the good of Christian fasting?

Gifts for the poor can be sent to: Fr. Basil, Food for the Poor, 1301 W. Copans Road, Pompano Beach, FL 33064.

And Still We Are Tempted

Saint Benedict uses many different images in describing the monk: he is a soldier doing battle for Christ, our true King; he is a student in the school of the Lord's service; he is a son and heir in the household of the Paterfamilias; he is a craftsman laboring in the workshop of the enclosure. In the fourth chapter of his Rule, he provides his craftsman with seventy-two tools for the spiritual craft. They include the ten commandments and counsels from Sacred Scripture. They also include much wisdom from the Fathers.

One of these tools is this: As soon as wrongful thoughts come into your heart, dash them against Christ, as against a rock, and disclose them to your spiritual father. Benedict, the true son of Antony, the Desert Father, knows what monsters these evil thoughts can become. Iconography and medieval hagiography have had great fun depicting the temptations of Anthony, but they were very real—as every monk comes to experience. So Benedict's advice is quite ruthless. He is undoubtedly thinking of the last verse of Psalm 137: A blessing on him who takes and dashes your little ones against the rock. The rock for

Saint Jerome
Holy Trinity Abbey
Huntsville, UT

us is, as Saint Paul said, Christ the Lord, the source of all grace. As Moses struck the rock in the desert and the people received life-giving water, so too, when we dash our temptations against Christ, his grace pours forth to sustain us. As soon as any evil thought arises in our hearts we want to cast it and ourselves at his feet and let the comfort of his love and friendship give us the satisfaction we are tempted to seek elsewhere.

Those who regularly practice Centering Prayer have an excellent tool for handling wrongful thoughts, whether they be actual temptations or just dissipating, useless or self-deprecating thoughts. With practice, our prayer word gains a great power to bring us to the center, to Christ. In the prayer, we have learned that whenever thoughts catch hold of us we can use the word to return to the center and let the thoughts flow away. So through the day when unwanted thoughts come upon us, instead of fighting them, which may well strengthen their presence, we can simply with our own prayer word go to the center for a moment and let the unwanted thought or feeling, the temptation, float away.

We are programmed to see temptations as something evil: Lead us not into temptation. It comes as a bit of a surprise then when we read in Saint Matthew's Gospel: "Jesus was led by the Spirit into the wilderness to be tempted by the devil." This is not quite what we would expect the Holy Spirit to do. Temptation insofar as it is an act of the evil one arising out of his envy and hatred is certainly evil. Insofar as it is the good things of the world enticing our disintegrated nature to act in insubordination, it is not good. But for those who love God, all things work together unto good. The challenge can make us grow, give us fuller insight, make us more like our Lord and Master, who struggled with temptation from the days in the wilderness till he hung naked on the cross and was buffeted with the cry: If you be the Son of God, come down. Thus Saint James could encourage the first Christians:

> My sisters and brothers, you will always have your temptations but, when they come, try to treat them as a happy privilege; you understand that your faith is truly put to the test to make you patient, but patience too is to have its practical results so that you will become fully developed, complete, with nothing missing.

Our Lord had gone into the desert to empty himself as completely as possible of the things of this world in order to be filled with the Spirit, to receive the sure guidance he needed for the mission and ministry that lay ahead. This is something of the meaning of novitiate in active religious institutes and seminary for diocesan priests, something that is perhaps being missed in our days: the need to go apart and really empty the self to be prepared. It was when

Christ had most completely emptied himself, even physically, and was most open to the Spirit that the evil spirit came upon him. We are sometimes surprised to hear of the temptations of holy ones. People sometimes think nuns and monks locked away in their cloisters are free from temptations. *Not at all.* It was in this the most monastic part of his life that Jesus was tempted. When we take our Christ-life seriously and make true efforts to be like him, the devil becomes more interested in us. When we most open ourselves to the Holy Spirit, the evil spirit, the deceiver, using the very words of Scripture, seeks to insinuate himself.

The devil tried to snare Christ with very literal interpretations of Scripture. This might warn us to beware of making too much of individual texts as words from the Lord. We need always to place them in the context of the whole Revelation and above all in the context of the two great commandments.

Christ, our model, faced the onslaughts of the evil one first in regard to the basic drives of human life: food and power—control over one's own life and control over others and the situations of life.

The temptations were very real. Christ was a hungry man. The sight and smell, the comforting feeling of fresh bread in his empty stomach quickly arose in his imagination. But not by bread alone does one live, but by every word that comes forth from the mouth of God. Fasting does create in us a hunger, a hunger that can be sublimated into a deep longing for

God and for his Revelation. The well-fed are often sluggish at their *lectio*. They are content. There is no incarnation of their spiritual hunger. There are always vast spaces in our spirit longing for God, but we can be very much out of touch with them if we are too intent upon satisfying ourselves on more superficial levels. Having the courage to deny some of these needs, we can attend more freely to feeding the spirit. The monk then does not dwell on his empty tummy but on his empty spirit and lets the hunger he experiences drive him on to a *lectio* that is filled with a greater hunger for God.

Monastic life is in many ways very humdrum, very prosaic. There is an established routine that goes on day after day. The faithful monk's longing for God does grow. There is the temptation to step out of the routine and take some mighty leap in faith, a short cut that will call forth a surge of divine power in this painfully slow work of purification and sanctification. The last words written by the Patriarch of the West, flowing out of years of experience, are these: "Through patience we share in the passion of Christ"—patience with God, patience with ourselves, patience with everyone else. The temptation to be impatient, to try to force the hand of God is great, the temptation to do things our "brilliant" and "efficient" way rather than letting him work in us through the slowly paced circumstances of daily life and daily fidelity. "You must not tempt the Lord your God." We must let him do it his way and cooperate as best we can, trusting that he will indeed complete the work when it is to be completed and not one moment before. He has everything under control. Sufficient for the day is the evil thereof.

When we have struggled with temptations and by God's grace been freed from them, we experience a certain spiritual power. It is something of the power that came upon Moses and Elijah and Christ himself after their fasts and struggles. We should not be too quick to expect this to be a permanent state nor too surprised if temptations do return. God often gives us seasons of respite before the final struggle. We can enjoy the season of grace but hold it with gentleness and dispossessiveness.

With spiritual power a new temptation can move upon us, the third temptation. All things are ours: "All things are yours and you are Christ's and Christ is God's." But we can become possessive, dominating, judgmental. We have overcome temptation, we have put a restraint on ourselves, our passions, our emotions; why shouldn't everyone else? The Fathers tell this story:

> One day one of the younger brothers was caught in fornication. The elders gathered to judge him and expel him from the community. But Abba Moses did not come. The elders sent for him, insisting he come. Finally, the old man did come, carrying on his back a large basket of sand in which he had

poked a hole. The sand trailed behind him. "Should I come and sit in judgment on a brother when my own sins trail behind me?"

In the litanies we pray: "For peace and compunction all the days of our lives." Compunction, an abiding sorrow for our sins, is a great liberating spirit. It keeps us humbly grateful that we have been freed from our sins. It wards off the temptation to judge others in whom the Lord has not yet brought this about. We accept the Lord God as the sole supreme master of this creation and fully accept his way of working in each of his servants. That he has freed us and works powerfully in us, we rejoice. At the same time we fully accept the limitations of the power he has given us in the Spirit.

This power is especially a power for compassion. Christ is able to be compassionate with us, the Scriptures tell us, because of the things he suffered. So, too, having gone through temptations ourselves and knowing that we have overcome in the end only by his power, we can have compassion on our brothers and sisters who struggle. We can assure them with Saint Paul: "The temptations you have to bear are no more than people normally have. You can trust God not to let you be tried beyond your strength, and with any trial he will give you a way out of it and the strength to bear it."

There is a very powerful help in overcoming

temptation, and it is one that monasticism has always held in the highest regard. It is part of the tool Saint Benedict hands to his disciple: "And disclose the temptation to your spiritual father." There are a number of factors that come into play here. First of all, bringing our temptations out into the light fully unmasks them. We see more clearly the deceptions they cloak. Very shame supports us in saying no to them. We are strengthened by the support of our father's prayer and the knowledge of his prayer and care. We are not alone in facing the enemy of our souls. But there is another element. We should lay before our father all our thoughts and inspirations (especially those we are most tempted to conceal) for sometimes temptation is so subtly presented by the evil one that we can mistake it for a good inspiration. Bringing all to the father, we can receive advice, counsel and enlightenment.

It is not always easy for a lay person to find a spiritual father or mother or even a companion for the journey. But if one truly seeks one will find. It is well worth the search and I would strongly urge it. The hope to make real progress in the Christ-life without a guide or companion on the journey is almost an illusion. God can, of course, directly and immediately provide all the guidance a person needs. He is not bound to any particular way of doing things. Yet it is his most common way to guide us through one another, to have us pilgrims assist each other. We should be slow to conclude it is to be otherwise with ourselves. Rather, we should make every effort to establish a supportive relationship with a spiritual mother or father or friend who can walk with us on the way. It is a real grace we offer another when we invite someone to help us in this way, for the Lord in response to our faith will give that person all the graces we need and he or she too will profit from them.

Temptation is a part of every Christian life. Monastic tradition gives us a simple response to it: As quickly as possible, as soon as we perceive it, dash it against Christ and let it be exposed to the light. It is not something to play around with; we must not tempt the Lord our God. We must not deny its danger or begin to rationalize as we are so prone to do. Rather we must turn to the sustaining Word of God and, giving ourselves in homage to him, acknowledge in the fabric of our being that he is the Lord our God, and him alone do we serve, not our own desires. We take up our daily cross, for we have the privilege of being his disciples. Like him we are tempted so that like him we may, through a dying to self, come to the freedom of the risen life.

Men and Women of Peace

*T*here was a great calm and peacefulness as the Patriarch sat in his usual spot before the gate of the monastery—quite different from yesterday. Then there were rumors, followed by messengers with the fateful news: Tutila, the Goth, was on his way. The people from the surrounding villages flocked up the mountain to consult their beloved father. Not too many listened to his quiet, assuring words of peace. Most had fled. And now the village and mountain was still, a land deserted. Abbot Benedict's own monks moved about quietly in the depths of the great abbey, their actions filled with a more intense prayer. The hour was perilous indeed and heaven was to be implored. But, by and large, the monks shared the quiet faith and peace that flowed from their father.

Then rumbling could be heard, first in the distance but rapidly coming closer. A dust cloud rose above the dry road from the north. It was a while before precise figures emerged. The horde came rushing onward, lured by the fabled wealth of the great abbey on the hilltop. Soon they were ascending the steep mountain road. The father sat there serenely, as he did each day after lunch, to receive the

Cloister
New Clairvaux Abbey
Vina, CA

petitions of the people. The somewhat less confident brothers gathered in the inmost depths of the immense building, huddled together in fervent prayer. Their loving support was with him.

In the end the feared Goth, awed by the sanctity of the monk, fell prostrate in his presence. It would be wonderful to know the thoughts and feelings and emotions that raced through him in this moment of encounter. All history tells us is that when he remounted he went away in peace and was from that time on far less cruel.

When Louis VII of France and Geoffrey Plantagenet sat confronting each other in the large striped tent in the fields outside of Paris, the prospects for peace seemed very dim. The armies were animated with ambition and pride. The tent flap opened and a diminutive man in a long gray robe entered. In a moment the king of France was prostrate, the pretender of England on his knees. It was Bernard, the abbot of Clairvaux. When the monk left the tent, the lords knew they were brothers, a pact had been drawn and signed; the English pretender returned to his home in peace.

Monks have always been ministers of peace from the days of the great Antony, who emerged from the desert, through the days of Peter of Tarentaise, who stood before the Barbarossa, right up to our own times. In all the turmoil of Vietnam the Buddhist monks and their Catholic brothers from the Cistercian communities consistently stood for peace.

And when a certain peace came to their own land they set out on a World Peace March to call all to that level of consciousness which can lead a nuclear society into true and lasting peace.

The call of the Christian to be a peacemaker is clear and unequivocal. We are called to follow Christ to be his disciples. And he is the Prince of Peace. He is the Son of God and it is the peacemakers who will be called sons and daughters of God. The danger is that we Christians in our peacemaking efforts will be drawn to interact at a secular or materialistic level, working only at economics and politics, and not make the unique contribution we can as persons of faith, empowered in oneness with Christ, creating the context for true and lasting peace. Saint Peter warns us: "Be on your guard lest you be led astray by the error of the wicked and forfeit the security you enjoy."

Benedict and Bernard and the other true monastic peacemakers of history have been effective because they have acted from a deep source of peace within themselves, creating a context for peace. This is the contribution a Christian woman or man of peace can make. While the churches can and should mobilize their vast, well-organized structures for the peace effort and exert considerable economic and political influence, their most proper contribution will be at the level of the spirit. Women and men of the Church, along with those of other spiritual traditions, can bring a special contribution. Opening ourselves to allow the Spirit to create in us her fruit of peace, the peace that flows from love, we can become true sources of peace.

As Benedict and Bernard, nuns and monks are persons of peace because a certain asceticism frees them from the violence of their own passions. This does not mean that nuns and monks no longer have emotions, no longer experience love and anger, no longer are touched by the stirrings of ambition, vengefulness, lust. But a practiced asceticism teaches monastics to recognize and accept these movements and then decide what to do with them: let them go while proceeding to what they really want to do; use them to energize a response to the situation; sublimate them into their opposite or other directions.

The nun and monk through the contemplative experience, which enables them to see themselves reflected in the eyes of God, know themselves. Only God can fully comprehend the beauty of the persons he has made, for he has made us in his image and likeness. When we come to know our own beauty, our value, our being in God, we are eminently free in the face of what others think and say, how they evaluate us. It is not that the monastics do not seek support and appreciation of others. For this we enter into a community of love. We want it and we seek it, for we are greatly helped by it—just like everyone else. But we are not dependent upon it. Therefore, it does not dictate our actions. We can say and do what we know we should with great peace, for we are not dependent upon the acceptance of others. We act out of the Source, the center where we are always coming forth from the infinite and all-affirming love of God.

Our *lectio*, our listening engenders in us a deep faith—faith comes from hearing. We know we have not here a lasting dwelling place, we are en route, we are pilgrims. With death, life is not ended but changed. And so, even in the face of death, we can be at peace, like Saint Benedict sitting at the gates of Monte Cassino. Death had lost its sting. We are free in the face of death because we have put our stock in the deeper, unending life of the Spirit. This does not mean we do not value life. Knowing all life from its Source, we savor life far more fully than one who clings to it with anxiety. We know the sacredness of life, the quality it should have, and we seek to promote that. Visitors to most monasteries are struck by the beauty of the monastic domain, the good life the monks live, the warmth of the hospitality, the reverence shown to guests, the prevailing peace.

The experience of God, whom we constantly seek, the Source of all life, who has all things in his loving fatherly hands, leaves us secure and at peace, even in the face of nuclear holocaust. "He's got the whole wide world in his hand." God does have everything under control. His thoughts are not always our thoughts, nor our ways his ways. But in the end, his will will be done on earth as in heaven.

There is a constant danger of our forgetting this, at least in practice, and acting and strategizing as

124

though all depended upon us. In God's design much does depend on us. We have our responsibility—our ability to respond to his call and leadership and participate in the creation of a new heaven and a new earth. But we can be at peace if we remember: results are his business. "One sows, another waters, God gives the increase." We can be profoundly at peace and create a context of peace for others, surrounding them with caring love and listening attentively to the communication of their hearts if we ourselves are in touch with the Source of peace and are acting out of that Source.

We can do this by regularly making time to let everything else go and rest in the Source at the center of our being (which we can do through Centering Prayer or any other legitimate method of meditation). Making time and letting things go, even our own thoughts, feelings and desires, is a real asceticism that sets us free and leaves us at peace. The experience of God and of our own beauty in God enables us to act with great freedom and love. We can create the space within which others can discover their own beauty and power. They can let go of their defensiveness and get in touch with their true aspirations, realizing the oneness and the basic aspirations shared by all fellow-travelers on this globe.

The contemplative experience of God, Creator of All, understood through the teaching of our Master, the Prince of Peace, is the powerful and unique contribution that we can bring to a threatened world.

Universal caring and sharing, because we are all one in our Source, will lead to a world where there will be no one to fight, no one to arm against, none of the injustices that cry out for vengeance. In a word they will lead to a new level of consciousness.

We desperately need this new level of consciousness. Never has it been known in the history of nations that a people have stockpiled weapons and have not used them. But if we use our stockpiles we will not be here long enough to know it—nor will anyone else. We have to break with this pattern of the past and create a new pattern. We have to be free enough to destroy our own weapons, free enough to go beyond where we are and find a new mode of security in a prevailing climate of oneness and trust, of human solidarity. Is there really any hope we can do this as a global people?

Prayer can be effective of this through its intercessory power, harnessing the creative energy which is presently bringing forth the hearts of us all. The same God who hardened the heart of Pharaoh can soften the hearts of today's leaders and of all of us. He can form in us new hearts. When God creates he does not abandon his creation; he doesn't make something, set it on its own feet, and walk away, as might a human carpenter. What he makes exists because at each moment he shares with it something of his own unique being. If he turned his attention from it, it would cease to exist. God is constantly bringing forth all that is. And he has willed that the way he brings it forth is in part determined by us: "Ask and it shall be done for you." This is the intercessory power of our prayer. It can bring about a global transformation through the divine, ever-active creative power of our God.

Prayer can also be effective through the transformation of consciousness it effects in us the prayers (we cannot constantly pray for peace and meditate on peace and not become more profoundly men and women of peace) and through us the rest of our species. The idea that the consciousness of one person can affect that of others is not new, that the transformation of consciousness of some can affect the whole. It is the leaven of the Gospel parable that leavens the whole. It is the attainment of Teilhard de Chardin's noosphere. It is not primarily quantity that makes the difference, it is quality. In prayer, in meditation, we take on more and more the mind of Christ, the Prince of Peace, the peacemaker par excellence. "For in him is our peace." We see the awesomeness of all life. The reverence that is the basis of a true ecology, of just stewardship, comes to possess us. Through prayer, our consciousness is transformed and because of the intimate interconnection of all human persons we become instruments in that transformation of consciousness that will set the human family on another course of action. Prayer will put us into intimate contact with the Source of all peace. It will establish peace in us. We will act out of the center of peace. We will have an invincible hope because it will be grounded on an unconquerable faith.

Even in the face of an apparently total catastrophe there is still cause for hope. Christ was destroyed on the cross and rose again. A new earth and God's full justice is to come to us. If we are tempted to lose patience with the apparently ceaseless and senseless arms race, "consider that our Lord's patience is directed toward salvation." Rather than being "led astray by the error of the wicked," by the idolatry that puts its hope in arms, we need to grow "in the knowledge of our Lord and Savior Jesus Christ" so that we can see that he is working in and through all. We do this through prayer.

I do not emphasize prayer here to downplay the importance of other activities and efforts for disarmament and the pursuit of universal peace in justice and love. God does work in and through the activities and efforts of women and men. But we cannot sustain such activities and efforts if we do not have hope. Prayer renews our faith and lets us powerfully experience that we do have cause for hope.

When we have convictions in regard to the power of a life that is centered to create peace, we can then, as peacemakers, seek to open this dimension of peace to others. We can share this aspect of the Christian tradition by sharing Centering Prayer or other forms of Christian meditation, forming meditation groups, introducing periods of meditative prayer into our meetings and rallies. If we act out of this source, then our activities will be peaceful, creating a context of peace and not engender any of the hostility or perpetuate any of the violence from which we seek to free ourselves and our global family.

Act we must. True love and concern postulate it. And there are many forms our activity can take besides propagating a contemplative approach to life which sources true peace. Recently the president of a multinational wrote with great frankness: "They (the Soviets) wouldn't even have been in the arms race had it not been for the incredible volume of loans made directly to the Soviet Union by U.S. banks . . . we continue to throw good money after bad. . . ." Besides praying for those who make the decisions in the great banking and trading corporation that they may use their power more creatively for peace, we can hold stock in such corporations and animate stockholders' interest to monitor and direct their activity. We can effectively support boycotts. We can use the media to protest the activities of war and support those of peace. We can seek direct communication with persons whose ideology or nationality is labeled "the enemy."

This does not seem to me to be the place to catalogue a long list of things to do or that can be done. As a spiritual community, a community inspired by the Spirit of Christ, we can make our essential contribution of creating a context for peace. Then we can count on the Holy Spirit to guide us in concrete activities in our own lives and in the life of our communities. We can seek peace and pursue it. Realizing we are each presently at different places, each with our own unique role, we can all pledge ourselves to depth, to openness, to readiness, to take the next step in faithfulness, to be blessed peacemakers, true daughters and sons of our God of Peace.

Friends

"*H*e must grow greater, I must grow smaller." Not smaller in the sense of any diminishment of my being or personhood, of what really matters, of who I am, but only in comparison to who he is, only in regard to anything in my person or in my activity that would impede his increase in me, in himself, in all. This is true love, true friendship. The beloved is placed first. His well-being, his growth, his glory is the concern, the desire. John Fortunato has defined love as "transcending one's self for the purpose of nurturing . . . another's spiritual growth." I like this definition.

Saint John Baptist is considered a special patron and model for monks. This is brought out in Byzantine monastic churches by the special place he is given on the iconostasis. There is first of all the icon of Christ, the Pantocrator, the Maker of All; then that of Mary, the Panaghia, the All-Holy One; then that of the particular patron of the monastery, and finally that of the Prodromos, the Forerunner, John the Baptizer. The choice seems logical enough. We think of John's life in solitude: "He lived out in the wilderness." We think of his austerity: "John wore a gar-

End of worktime
Saint Joseph's Abbey
Spencer, MA

ment of camel-skin." And of his fasting and abstinence: "He lived on locusts and wild honey." We
think of his prophetic witness: "Prepare a way for the
Lord, make his paths straight." He was indeed "the
voice of one crying in the wilderness." He did come
"not eating or drinking." We can well see him as a
model of these qualities. But the most beautiful and
significant description that John gives of himself does
not center on one of these. It is rather his description
of himself as *friend*. He was "the bridegroom's friend,
who stands and listens, is glad when he hears the
bridegroom's voice." He did indeed listen. Even
when the Bridegroom was still hidden in his Mother's
womb, when both of them were so hidden, John already heard his Bridegroom's voice in the voice of
Mary, his Bridegroom's Mother, and John leaped for
joy. He listened and was led by his Friend's Spirit.
Elsewhere in this volume I have spoken about listening. Here I want to speak about friendship. For in his
friendship, even more than in all his other qualities—
which indeed were all in service of his friendship—
John is our model.

On the night before he died, as he poured out his
heart and revealed the deepest meaning of his mission and his relation with us, Jesus said to us: "You
are my friends. . . . I shall not call you servants any
longer. . . . I call you friends." He expressed his
friendship by coming to be with us and abiding with
us: "And know that I am with you always, yes, to the
end of time." He shares with us all his secrets: "I have

made known to you everything I have learned from my Father." And finally, "A man can have no greater love than to lay down his life for his friends," and this he did for us.

The monk in his choice of celibacy, in saying "yes" to the call, the invitation, to embrace the life of a monk, chooses to be a friend of the Friend, to make that friendship the central reality of his life. And he enters a community of friends, a "school of love," in order to learn through friendship how to be a friend —in order to be a friend to the Friend because "whatever you do to the least of my brethren you do to me."

One of the most beautiful pictures of monastic mythology is that of Saints Antony and Paul meeting in the desert. Antony, the Father of Monasticism, and Paul the Hermit had long striven to live as true monks. They had heard of each other, had been encouraged and strengthened in their resolve by each other's example and prayer. At length, moved by the Spirit, Antony knew it was time to seek out his friend. In the loving embrace of these two is epitomized the meaning of monastic friendship. The friendships of youth are very beautiful, exciting, full of promise. But in the embrace of two old friends we see the fulfillment of some of our deepest aspirations.

I shall never forget the day Brother Thomas, after years as an oblate, made his solemn vows and was formally received into the monastic community. Age had already slowed him down a good bit and his eyesight was diminished. After all the monks in choir had gone up to embrace him to welcome him into the bosom of the community, Tom went in search of Brother Alfred. Ninety years young, nearly blind, "Uncle Alf" usually sat quietly in a corner during the services. Brother Tom knew he was there. At his approach, Alfred came out of his corner, and these two beautiful old men, slowed by age, groping as do the blind, came together in the middle of choir and embraced. Even as I write this my eyes fill with tears. There were few dry eyes in the choir that day. Paul and Antony were meeting again.

Monastic history is scored by wonderful friendships. My own blessed patron, Basil, had his school chum, Gregory. With youthful enthusiasm they set out together on the monastic quest. Later they were called forth from their monastery to be archbishops. They had their disagreements at times, but a magnificent eulogy gives witness to the ultimate triumph of friendship. Saint John Cassian had his dear Herman who shared his long search in the desert. There is the beautiful story of sister and brother, Scholastica and Benedict. When the day was not long enough for their sharing, heavenly rains blessed its prolongation through the night. Even death did not separate them as they shared a common tomb. So many monastic friendships could be recalled. Malachy of Ireland had his prayer answered when he died in the arms of his friend, Bernard of Clairvaux, so that their relics could be mingled in a common grave. Bernard was a man who knew friendship in its fullest. The letters exchanged between him and William of Saint Thierry, his closest friend, are embarrassingly naked, almost passionate. It was at Bernard's direction that Aelred of Rievaulx wrote as the primer of Cistercian life a *Mirror of Charity* which powerfully extols the beauty of friendship, warns wisely of its dangers and finds its consummation in mystic friendship within the Trinity. Let me quote just one of its more beautiful passages:

> It is such a great joy to have the consolation of someone's affection—someone to whom we are deeply united by the bonds of love, someone in whom our weary spirit may find rest, and to whom we may pour out our souls . . . someone whose conversation is as sweet as a song in the tedium of our daily life. He must be someone whose soul will be to us a refuge to creep into when the world is altogether too much for us, someone to whom we can confide all our thoughts. His spirit will give us the comforting kiss that heals all the sickness of our preoccupied hearts. He will weep with us when we are troubled and rejoice with us when we are happy; he will always be there to consult when we are in doubt. We will be so deeply bound to him in our hearts that even when he is far away, we shall find him together

with us in spirit, together and alone. The world will fall asleep around us, we will find, and our souls will be at rest, embraced in absolute peace. Our two hearts will be quiet together, united as if they were one, as the grace of the Holy Spirit flows over us both.

This work of his early years was not enough for Aelred. He continued it in a lifetime dialogue with his disciples the fruit of which he shares with us in his book *On Spiritual Friendship.*

In the centuries following Aelred, monasticism for the most part lost sight of this precious element of its heritage. Monks still gathered in communities. Charity was still extolled as the virtue par excellence. But friendship lost its place and even became suspect. There were various reasons for this.

One was the drive to get things done. Monks repeatedly became doers; ecclesiastical doers with parishes, missions, shrines and schools; material doers, too, with buildings and farms, trade and even industries. There was hardly enough time for minimal friendship with God in prayer, no time to relax and be with brothers in that present sharing that creates friendship. Jesus made time to be alone with his disciples: "You must come away to a lonely place all by yourselves and rest for a while." Even though there was a world to be saved there was time and space for friends.

As monasticism moved into the modern era, there was something of "throwing out the baby with the bath." There were failures in regard to friendship and lamentable lapses. Monks are men, and sinful men at that. Passion can and has overtaken them. Not all monks are necessarily "straight." They have experienced crushes, attachments, the distractions of love too human and other failures. Aelred had warned of all this. "Friendship is the most dangerous of all our affections." The Fathers who, like this Saint of Rievaulx, extolled monastic friendship were not oblivious to these dangers. But a later age in seeking to get rid of the pollutions pretty much did away with the beautiful reality. "Particular friendship"—and therefore all friendship, for every friend is particular —became suspect and proscribed.

Some have lamented this, but in fact not all that many. Even in these days of relatively enlightened renewal, when most monks have full freedom to develop deep friendships, relatively few do. The rigorous demands of true friendship, the gift of oneself, one's time, one's preference, the nakedness and honesty are beyond the price many are willing to pay— those who have not yet experienced what is purchased by such a price. Anyone who has been graced with true friendship knows the cost and knows the worth. And he knows, too, the ridiculousness of fear that such friendships will undermine community. It is, in truth, only the one who has been honed by true friendship who can give himself in fullness to communal love. True friends are the best community men.

Monks readily identify with the community to which they are attached by a solemn vow of stability. The ordinary circumstances of work and study develop comfortable acquaintances. But monastic structures usually fail to provide the time and the places which facilitate the development of intimate friendships. This is another cause of their absence. Aelred's beloved Ivo begged: "That as often as you visit your sons here, may I be permitted, at least once, to have you all to myself, to disclose to you the deep feelings of my heart without disturbances."

Christian communities are societies of friends— the Quakers have so well and beautifully realized— because we are called to be disciples of the Friend. Indeed, his one new commandment is to love as he has loved. It is not enough then to tolerate our fellows. We must truly love, transcend ourselves to nurture each other's spiritual growth.

The primary Christian community is the home. Here the basic attitude of wanting the other to increase, to grow greater, must be expressed in making time for each other. We affirm the other's worth and desirability by giving her or him priority when we allot our life's time. We have to take care, especially we men, that we do not let projects and doings, accomplishment and productivity squeeze out the gracious space of friendship. Like Christ, we have to make time and share—share the deepest things of our lives, "all that the Father has made known to me." This is what the "ten and ten" of Marriage Encounter is all about. We need to create structures that will facilitate the time, the space and true sharing in our home community. I am not necessarily speaking of a husband and wife here, but they should be friends par excellence, for it is their sublime vocation to sacramentalize for all of us the love of Christ, the Friend and Lover, for his Church and the love we the Church should have for him.

It takes a lot of courage to share with another what the Father is saying to us in our deepest conscience. And a bit of humility. But it is a powerful aid to being true to our truest self. And such sharing undercuts some of the deepest roots of our loneliness and our self-depreciation.

We may say there is no one in our community who would want to share with us at this level, no one whom we can so trust. That may be so now. The fact may be, no one would want so to trust us. But, in fact, such sharing, such friendship responds to a deep desire in all of us. Most of us are blocked by fears. True friendship doesn't just happen. We have to make time for it, cultivate it, gradually open ourselves and mutually uncover successive levels, till at last the light of love can shine into the very depths, and we can rejoice in our shared beauty in complete freedom. It takes a conviction that love and friendship are worth it. The full enjoyment of such a relationship may be long in coming, but even with the first stage the fruits are tasted and the hope and promise are great.

Friendship does not just happen, nor can it be forced; it is a gift—but a gift that must be accepted and cultivated. To *have* a friend, we must *be* a friend. We must turn from looking at faults—something we are strongly programmed to do in this competitive society of ours—to looking at strengths, beauty, gifts and talents. The faults and weaknesses must be accepted, too, with a loving, concerned and healing compassion. Our friendship must be treasured and protected, displayed, not easily given away, put in jeopardy or abused. We have to channel a lot of time and energy into a developing friendship. In this respect it may be initially truncating in regard to the development of other aspects of our lives. But as we call forth our friend we lay the foundation of further empowerment and support. A true friend becomes for us an icon of Christ, a special shrine where we find and love Christ and experience Christ's love for us.

Particular friendship is at the heart of our lives as Christians no matter what our call. It is when we are willing to walk all the way with our particular friend that we develop the self-transcending love that enables us to give ourselves in Christ-like love to all. It is

in the experience of deep, full, rich human love that
we begin to get some real insight into the intimacy to
which the Lord, our divine Friend, is calling us. "I
shall not call you servants anymore. . . . I call you
friends."

Sons and Daughters
of a Mother

*I*n Byzantine architecture the "royal doors" separate the sanctuary from the nave of the church, reminiscent of the veil of the temple in Jerusalem. But unlike the veil, which hides a place of fullest but unrevealed mystery and hung there in transcendent silence, the royal doors which open to bring forth the Incarnate God in sacred Communion set forth the images of the bearers of the Good News. The four Evangelists are depicted on their respective panels. Over and above them is Gabriel bearing glad tidings to Mary, the Maiden. Mary was the first to receive the Good News of the Incarnation, and in receiving it and accepting it, in God's design she helped to bring it about. Christ-God received his incarnation, his humanity, his blood relationship with us in and through her.

Saint Leo the Great (+461), sharing the voice of the Fathers of the Church, tells us that Mary in becoming the mother of the Head (taking up the Pauline theology of the Mystical Body of Christ) mothered also all his members. Some of the Fathers have

Native American madonna
Christ in the Desert
Albiquiu, NM

used the less gracious image of the neck—Mary is the "neck" of the Mystical Body. What they are saying is that all that comes to us from Christ, the Head of the Body, comes to us through Mary, the neck of the Body. Mary is the mediatrix of all graces. She was the way by which our Mediator descended from heaven to us. She collaborated with him in the first hours of his salvific mission and has never left off that collaboration. All from Jesus through Mary.

Monks have always been men of their times, even while they stepped outside of their times in quest of the transcendent and eternal. The medieval Cistercians were no exception. And their Marian piety is marked by the social structures and outlook of that period. Knowing that all comes through Mary, they saw their monasteries as belonging to her as their Lady, the Mother and Consort of their Lord. All their monasteries bore her name, along with that of the locale: the Monastery of Blessed Mary of the Valley of Light (Clairvaux); the Monastery of Blessed Mary of the Beautiful Fountain (Bellefontaine), the Monastery of Blessed Mary of the Seven Fountains (Sept Fons). The monks—when they entered the monastic community and took up residence in her house—became her vassals and took her name, usually along with that of one of her great servants. In acknowledgment of their filial fiefdom, each evening they ended their day's service with the solemn chant, "Hail, Holy Queen." These practices continue to be a part of the living heritage of the Cistercian monks and nuns today in all parts of the world.

I have known Mary as my Mother since I first came to know her at my mother's knee. My earthly mother, now in heaven, told me of my heavenly Mother and was a sacrament of her love and care. Grandma taught me the rosary at an early age. The beads I had seen so often in her fingers had fascinated me. In the school of the rosary I came to know my Mother and in the May and October devotions and in the living of the liturgical year from the feast of the Immaculate Conception and the birth of the Virgin to the Annunciation, Visitation and Nativity of the Lord on through the Passion to the glories of the Assumption. In the monastery liturgical readings and personal *lectio* brought me the reflective faith and rich theology of the Fathers and the monastic tradition. I came to know more (and it is still growing) the sublimity of "our tainted nature's solitary boast." I experienced more her mediation and in this her intimate closeness. Her virginal freedom and complete dispossessiveness that enabled her to be pure gift have called me. Her brave exile has encouraged me in my going apart from others. Her unjust persecution with her hunted Son and her identification with the condemned crucified One have enabled me to accept the daily contradictions and to identify more fully with my persecuted and suffering sisters and brothers. Her complete "yes" constantly challenges me. I want—by her example and mediation—to be like her Son a "yes" to the Father.

The fact that our monasteries actually belong to Mary is concretely acknowledged by the presence of her image—a window, statue or painting—in a most prominent place in the church, usually above the principal altar. As the day's services conclude, candles are lit before the image and all other lights fade out. For a few moments all attention is focused on Mary and one of the most solemn, beautiful and beloved chants, the *Salve Regina* (Hail, Holy Queen), is sung to her. Then, for the third time in the course of the day, a special bell calls us to a special prayer.

The bell in our belfry, modest though it be, sends across the hills three strokes of three. Each time this happens in the monastic day, all comes to a standstill; some kneel, some prostrate. And we live again in sacramental mystery that most awesome moment in salvation history when

> The angel of the Lord declared unto Mary,
> And she conceived of the Holy Spirit.
>   (Reflect for the space of an *Ave*—Hail Mary)
> Behold the handmaid of the Lord,
> Be it done unto me according to your word.
>   (Reflection)
> The Word was made flesh
> And dwelt among us.
>   (Reflection)

And then as the bell rings out, we pray:

Pray for us, O holy Mother of God,
That we may be made worthy of the promises of
   Christ.

> Pour forth we beseech you, O Lord, your
> grace into our hearts, that we to whom the
> Incarnation of Christ your Son was made
> known by the message of an angel, may by
> his passion and death be brought to the
> glory of his resurrection. Through the same
> Jesus Christ, our Lord. Amen.

It is the ancient practice of the *Angelus,* depicted in
Millet's memorable painting.

The bell falls silent, the prayer is completed. The
monks file silently toward the dormitory. A percep-
tive observer can notice a certain stirring within the
monk's long sleeves and perhaps hear a gentle rattle
of beads. As they go about the monastery, most often
monks finger the beads—Mary's rosary.

Some of the most beautiful images I have of my
brother monks arise now. I think of old Brother
Alfred, ninety years young, shuffling down the road
all but hidden under his broad-brimmed straw hat, a
sturdy cane in one hand and the rosary prominently
in the other. Indeed, I can hardly remember a time
when I have met Brother and he didn't have the rosary in hand. Brother Stan, our Polish wrestler, the

same. His rosary had so many medals attached to it we could always hear him coming.

The rosary stays in the monk's hand as he falls off to sleep. It is often in his hand during the day as he prays and meditates. He trusts it will be in his hand when Mary prays for him "at the hour of our death," and his brothers lay him gently on the boughs of spruce at the bottom of his grave.

Each home can certainly profit not only by a dedication that will place it securely under the special care of the Mother of all but also by her presence therein, symbolized by a worthy shrine. Those who enter the home of a devout Orthodox Christian are immediately greeted by the holy icons enshrined in the corner facing the entry. They bring a real Presence to the home and family and all visitors. Mary's image can do the same for us. Such a presence will invite the family at significant moments—how good it would be if it were each evening—to gather around. The house and all its blessings come from God through her. From her comes the strength to bear the burdens and trials. She, the Mother, can gather the children together when humanness drives them apart. She can watch over those absent, far and near.

There can, of course, be other times and places of prayer and gratitude. The Angelus, that thrice daily commemoration of the Incarnation, is an especially beautiful practice. While thanking God for this most precious of all his gifts, I find my hope, confidence and joy constantly renewed by this prayer. It is something different each time. It is a touching of the substance of what is. Not to allow ourselves these moments open to the fulfillment of all we long for and desire, not to structure such moments into our daily lives, is to cheat ourselves of so much that is rightfully ours.

And then there are the "beads," the rosary. It doesn't take long to pray the rosary—ten or fifteen minutes is ample. But we don't have to wait till we have even that bit of time. If we carry the beads in a pocket or keep them nearby we can finger them any free moment. As the monk prays his beads while walking down the cloister or the path to work or upstairs, so the beads can be the prayer of passing moments. In fact, no word need be said, nor specific thought—the touch of the fingers can be the silent heartfelt outreach to God through and with Mary.

As we pray the rosary more formally, we ponder the most intimate mysteries of our faith-life, with the Hail Mary as the quiet background. We ask Mary to lead us into that fullness of understanding that she ultimately found, through a lived participation and into that full sharing of the fruit of these saving mysteries that is preeminently hers in her complete freedom from sin and her corporeal glorification in the palace of her Son.

Mary is first because she sought to be last. Behold the handmaid, the servant, the slave girl, the one unworthy of motherhood. The monk seeks a way of life that is to be characterized, as Saint Benedict, the father of the monastic way, puts it, by zeal for *opprobria*—a desire for the humble and humbling way, so that he might mother Christ the better in himself and others. If we would be close to Mary in her greatness, we must be close to her in her lowliness. The life of each one of us is marked with the daily cross: pains, aches, humiliations. Mary points the hopeful way to rise from these with her Risen Son so that we might, with her, ascend to him in glory.

To this we all aspire, and may the Lord in his mercy bring us.

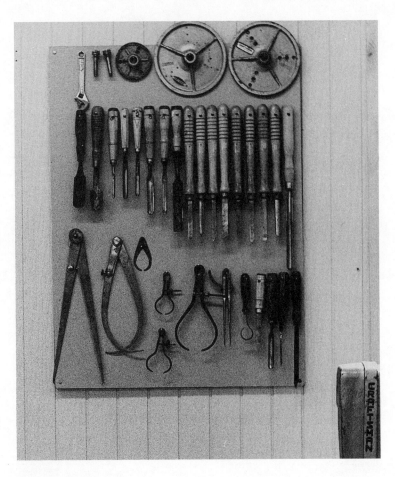

Carpenter shop
Genesee Abbey
Piffard, NY

Postscript

*O*ur country is blessed with many monasteries of nuns and monks. A visit to one, longer or shorter, can afford you the opportunity to experience more fully the values we have spoken about and, if you wish, receive assistance in integrating them into your own life. The Cistercian abbeys of the United States welcome you:

Assumption Abbey
Rt. 5 Box 193
Ava MO 65609
417-683-5110

Genesee Abbey
Piffard NY 14533
716-243-0660

Gethsemani Abbey
Trappist KY 40051
502-549-3117

Holy Cross Abbey
Berryville VA 22611
703-955-1424

Holy Spirit Abbey
Conyers GA 30207
404-483-8705

Holy Trinity Abbey
Huntsville UT 84317
801-745-3784

Mepkin Abbey
Moncks Corner SC
  29461
803-899-3428

Mount Saint Mary's
  Abbey*
Wrentham MA 02093
617-528-1282

New Clairvaux Abbey
Vina CA 96092
916-839-2161

New Melleray Abbey
Dubuque IA 52001
319-588-2319

Our Lady of the Angels
  Abbey*
Crozet VA 22932

Our Lady of Guadalupe
  Abbey
Box 97
Lafayette OR 97127
503-852-7174

Our Lady of the
  Mississippi Abbey*
Dubuque IA 52001
319-582-2595

Redwoods Abbey*
Whitethorn CA 95489
707-986-7419

Saint Benedict's Abbey
Snowmass CO 81654
303-927-3311

Saint Joseph's Abbey
Spencer MA 01562
508-885-3010

Santa Rita Abbey*
Box 97
Sonoita AZ 85637
602-455-5595

* Indicates monasteries of nuns.